Also by Dr. Yonnie Fowler:

Abigail: Becoming a Woman of Understanding

To God and to my Lord and Savior, Jesus the Christ. I thank my beloved companion, God's precious Holy Spirit, for inspiration and patient guidance throughout the writing of this book.

"Love is patient, love is kind" (1 Corinthians 13:4 NIV).

CONTENTS

INTRODUCTION

First Corinthians 13 is known as the love chapter, where Paul's first descriptive characteristic of love is patience. But what does patience have to do with love? The King James Version of the Bible uses the words *charity* and *long-suffering*, while other Bible versions have replaced *charity* with *love*, and *love that suffers long* is replaced with *patience*. Yet even if we say that love is patient, what does that mean? If I tolerate people or the very things that other people ignore and run away from, does that mean that I love more? And if I am able to suffer for a long time, does that make me a better Christian? Long-suffering does not suggest cowardice, nor does it imply a lack of pep. But only when we suffer long with love are we able to do what the Bible requires of us. "Love your enemies, bless them that curse you, do good to them that hate you, and pray for them which despitefully use you, and persecute you" (Matthew 5:44

KJV). Patience is one of the graces of love: "Love suffers long" (1 Corinthians 13:4 NKJV). Hate quickly condemns a wrong that is suffered, but love mitigates it with patience. Therefore, "Let us run with patience the race that is set before us" (Hebrews 12:1 KJV).

I am not a theology major, and the truths that I share concerning patience are not theological in the sense of the word; they are simply practical.

CHAPTER 1

LOVE IS PATIENT

"LOVE IS PATIENT" (1 CORINTHIANS 13:4 NIV). When Paul speaks of love, the very first thing he mentions is that it is patient. The Greek word for *patient* is *makrothymia*, which refers to a forbearing, persevering, patient love toward a person; a form of self-sacrificial love that is extended to someone else. Patience is essentially waiting with grace. Makrothymia is a fundamental character trait of God's.

Knowing who God is defines who we are. God is the very essence of love. No one knows what love is except in the self-revelation of God, and the revelation of God is Jesus Christ. God's love for humans became known in Jesus Christ. And when humans come to know Jesus Christ, they come to know God's love. Like begets like, and reaping depends on sowing. The principle of reciprocal love is stated in the Bible. "We love Him, because He first loved us" (1 John 4:19 KJV). Humankind gravitates toward love. To live apart from love, there is no joy. For if you live without love, you live a cold and heartless existence.

> Love is the director that brings together and reconciles the discordant notes in our jangling society and converts them into a beautiful harmony. Truly, love is the sweetest thing that ever grew in a human heart. Attesting to its breadth and length, depth and height, beauty and goodness, helpfulness and holiness, the very word picked by the Holy Spirit to describe God is love. John, inspired by the Holy Spirit, simply and briefly put it this way: "God is love." (1 John 4:8 KJV)[1]

He who loves most lives most. To attain the highest peak of living, one must not have a heart of hate, bitterness, or resentment but a heart of love.

Before God formed the earth, He was love. To describe love as being patient is saying that God is patient. The Bible tells us in Genesis 1:26 (KJV), "And God said, 'Let us make man in our image, after our likeness.'" Therefore, if God is love, and love is patient, and we are created in God's image, then we are created to be patient. God created us to be people who patiently take the time to look through heart lenses of love in order to see the best in others.

If we see ourselves through God's eyes, knowing our evil rebellion against His love and moral standards, still finding ourselves forgiven on the basis of Christ's death for us, then we will be set free to love others in imitation of God.

God loves us so much that He gives us the privilege of basking in His love. And it is only through basking—spending time with God—that we become like God. To paint a word picture of basking in love, I picture someone reclining on a summer day while soaking up the sunshine with a tall glass of lemonade. Actually, I like to think of this as the lazy, hazy days of summer. God is seen in all of nature. And although I have painted a picture of summer, God is seen in every season. He is personalized by the snowflake of winter, for it is said that no two snowflakes are alike. We see Him in springtime with all the newness of life as God shows Himself through the budding trees and the beautiful flowers that peek their heads up out of a ground that was recently covered with snow. We see Him in summers that are full of blissful childhood memories, and I dare not forget to mention the brilliant background foliage of fall that has been captured in so many paintings. God in all His wonder created the magnificent seasons. "Thou art worthy, O Lord, to receive glory and honor and power: for Thou hast created all things, and for Thy pleasure they are and were created" (Revelation

4:11 KJV). Sometimes we sprint through seasons with anticipation for what is next, only to realize that we never took the time to allow ourselves to be captivated by the beauty and awesomeness of God in the here and now, the present, forgetting that tomorrow is not promised to us.

How many times have we heard the words "Just be patient"? These words are spoken by parents to children who are trying to grow up too fast, or to the financial investor who wants to quickly see increase, or to the people who are stuck in slow-moving traffic when they are already running late, and to the young lady who has been waiting for a marriage proposal that she feels is long overdue. The list goes on and on. No matter how quickly we desire to see things happen, some things only happen at a snail's pace. Yet it is in these times that we must learn to be patient. The words "Just be patient" are meant to be spoken through hearts of love. No one wants to see their child rush into life without preparation or before pondering the cost. No one wants to see someone get caught in a get-rich-quick scam. No one wants to see someone hurry through traffic only to end up in an accident. And it's sometimes hard to see a young lady who seems to be so in love wait years for a marriage proposal, even when you know that the couple doesn't seem compatible. Love must always be the residing factor for patience.

I'm reminded of my grandchild when arriving at school with her mother during her first few days of kindergarten. She would cry for what seemed to be no reason other than what her mother thought was anxiety over her new environment. When her mother asked why she was crying, her response was that she felt rushed. Her mother decided that she would allow her daughter extra time in the morning to alleviate her rushed feelings, which in turn stopped the crying. In this instance, patience was shown through loving concern, exemplifying the fact that love is patient. "And the servant of the Lord must not strive; but be gentle unto all men, apt to teach, patient" (2 Timothy 2:24 KJV). There have been times in my life when I have felt rushed, just like my granddaughter. My internal feelings were not those of love. Rather, I felt that I was an annoyance. If we want to exemplify love, we must show patience toward others. "Now the God of patience and consolation grant you to be likeminded one toward another according to Christ Jesus" (Romans 15:5 KJV).

Marriage is thought of as two people being like-minded, yet the divorce rate of Christians is just as high as non-Christians. How can that be? Could it be that patience does not have a part in the marriage? If love is patient and two people come together in a marriage because they love each other, then patience must abide

5

within the marriage. Theologian Dietrich Bonhoeffer wrote in a letter for a marriage ceremony that he could not conduct due to his imprisonment for his failed attempted assassination of Adolf Hitler, "It is not your love that sustains your marriage, but from now on the marriage that sustains your love."[2] In other words, you are not married because you love each other, but you love each other because you are married. If marriage sustains love, and love is patient, then patience must be evident in a marriage. When it comes to marriage, some couples have very short wicks. Sometimes it appears as though they have vowed to put up with only so much rather than vowing to be patient with each other. It is often said between husband and wife, "I am not putting up with that." It is better to say, "I am letting go and letting God." God can handle what we cannot. In other words, God is able to put up with the things that we are not able to.

Marriage is designed to prepare us for heaven, but so many couples want to run from the preparation. "This is a great mystery: but I speak concerning Christ and the church" (Ephesians 5:32 KJV). Just as God wants us to relate to the church in love and not out of obligation, so it is in a marriage. Couples should relate to each other through love and not as a forced obligation. Paul said, "I have learned, in whatsoever state I am, therewith to be content"

(Philippians 4:11 KJV). Sometimes couples (or maybe one person in the marriage) may think life is greener on the other side, but when one hops over the fence, one finds that one was looking through green-colored glasses. Looking through the rearview mirror, the marriage that once was so terrible on the other side now looks pretty good from this view. And now families are torn apart. If one does not resolve one's issue of impatience, that same issue will reoccur wherever one may go. Now what was once a marital issue has turned into an anger issue. Children are angry, and they don't even know why. All they know is that Daddy or Mommy has left, and they blame themselves. They think their parents' breakup was their fault for. And if that is not enough, the child grows up and becomes an adult who needs the child within to be healed.

Even when someone reaches toward the sky with a shaking and clenched fist at God, His love does not stop. God still loves us. God does not love us on good days and despise us on our worst. God loves us unconditionally. We put stipulations on people—loving them *if*. If they act accordingly or if they meet whatever needs we require, then we will love them. But God does not love us depending on *if* we meet His conditions; God loves us regardless. We do not have to perform or try to be what we are not for God to love us. We do not have to dress up or put on a false face; God loves us despite our inabilities. God patiently loves us just for who we are. What an amazing way to feel loved.

Patience grows us, which is why patience is a virtue. As a child growing up, I remember that having patience was not always easy—waiting for dinner to be ready or waiting to go somewhere, especially when that somewhere involved doing something special. But then I grew older, and I was the one preparing dinner, and the wait was no longer hard. My patience had grown to another level. I was now the parent who was learning to be patient with an impatient child. "When I was a child, I spoke as a child, I understood as a child, I thought as a child: but when I became a man, I put away childish things" (1 Corinthians 13:11 KJV).

It is the same when we begin to grow up in Christ. Waiting, which was once hard, becomes less difficult. We at first think it strange when trials come. We ask the question, "Why, Lord?" Trials come to test our faith, and that is why we must go through trials rather than run from them. For, without a test, we will not have a testimony. It is through the trials of life that God holds us ever so close. He lovingly holds our hand, and sometimes God has to hold us by our wrist so that we will not try to squirm loose. God knows us, and He knows that the trials He has allowed in our lives have come to make us stronger. "What then shall we then say to these things? If God be for us, who can be against us? ... Nay, in all these things we are more than conquerors through Him that loved us" (Romans 8:31, 37 KJV).

Even though people may hurt us at times, the hurt is born easier with patience. The actual intense feeling of a hurt is more in the mind of the sufferer than in the act itself. That is why hurt affects people differently. A hurt may drive one person to commit suicide, while the other may grin, bear it, and throw it off. The very members of our family make mistakes. We are all human and in need of patience. We need it for relationships to work and to keep our own peace of mind and tranquility.

Patience is what overrides the body's desire to choke the living daylights out of someone who desperately needs it. Patience does not respond every time a fool speaks. It is patience that protects humankind from self-destruction. Humans, therefore, must not turn themselves into brutish savages that kill themselves by gnashing one another. I sometimes think that in the church, we destroy our own wounded. It is so contradictory of our own profession—outrageous and shocking. Human experience and scripture teach that this is destruction for both the destroyed and the destroyer. "But if ye bite and devour one another, take heed that ye be not consumed one of another" (Galatians 5:15 KJV). We have a responsibility to

9

treat one another with patient love. "Warn those who are unruly, comfort the fainthearted, uphold the weak, be patient with all" (1 Thessalonians 5:14 NKJV).

A patient spirit is needed for the development of the fruit of the Spirit. Other traits of love are a kind behavior, generosity, humbleness, courteousness, unselfishness, mild temperedness, honesty, sincerity, tolerance, believing, hopefulness, and continual endurance. More than three hundred years ago, Baptiste Poquelin said, "If everyone were clothed with integrity, if every heart were just, frank, kindly, the other virtues would be well-nigh useless, since their chief purpose is to make us bear with patience the injustice of our fellows."[3]

John Donne was famous for his poem "No Man Is an Island." God did not intend for us to live a hermit life, far away from imperfect people. People will sometimes judge us wrongly and treat us unfairly. But it is because of these very people that patience is needed. People are human; they are fallible and make mistakes. Therefore, patience is needed for everyone. God says in Revelation 2:2 (NKJV), "I know your works, and your labor, your patience." God sees every patient deed that is done, and He will reward those in whom patience is found.

I can always recall my mother saying, "Haste makes waste." I am reminded of a story told by Chuck Swindoll in his book *Come before Winter.*

> There was once a fellow who, with his dad, farmed a little piece of land. Several times of year they would load up the old ox-drawn cart with vegetables and go into the nearest city to sell their produce. Except for their name and the patch of ground, father and son had little in common. The old man believed in taking it easy. The boy was usually in a hurry—the go-getter type. One morning, bright and early, they hitched up the ox to the loaded cart and started on the long journey. The son figured that if they walked faster, kept going all day and night, they'd make market by early the next morning ...
> "Here's your uncle's place. Let's stop in and say hello." ... The boy fidgeted and fumed while the two old men laughed and talked away almost an hour. On the move again, the man took his turn leading the ox. As they approached a fork in the road, the father led the ox to the right. "The left is the shorter way," said the son. "I know it," replied the old man, "but this way is much prettier."
> ... The winding path led through graceful meadows, wildflowers, and along a rippling stream—all of which the young man missed as he churned within, preoccupied and boiling with anxiety ... "Let's sleep here," he sighed. "This is the last trip I'm taking with you," snapped the son. "You're more interested in watching sunsets and smelling flowers than in making money!" "Why, that's the nicest thing you've said in a long time," smiled the dad ... Before sunrise the young man

hurriedly shook his father awake. They hitched up and went on. About a mile down the road they happened upon another farmer—a total stranger—trying to pull his cart out of a ditch. "Let's give him a hand," whispered the old man ... We need to help others in need—don't forget that." The boy looked away in anger ... Suddenly, a great flash split the sky. What sounded like thunder followed. Beyond the hills, the sky grew dark. "Looks like a big rain in the city," said the old man ... It was late afternoon by the time they got to the hill overlooking the city. They stopped and stared down at it for a long, long time. Neither of them said a word. Finally, the young man put his hand on his father's shoulder and said, "I see what you mean, Dad." They turned their cart around and began to roll slowly away from what had once been the city of Hiroshima.[4]

Patience is a virtue through which God delivers us from hurt and harm. Yet the patience of Jesus is shown in a different light as His human emotion is exemplified in Mark 7:31-35, when Jesus lets out a sigh. The Bible tells us that Jesus left the vicinity of Tyre and went through Sidon, down to the Sea of Galilee and into the region of the Decapolis. There, some people brought to him a man who was deaf and could hardly talk, and they begged him to place His hand on the man. After He took him aside, away from the crowd, Jesus put his fingers into the man's ears. Then He spit and touched the man's tongue. He looked up to heaven and with a deep *sigh* said to him, "Ephphatha!" (which means, "Be opened"). At this, the man's ears were opened, his tongue was loosened, and he began to speak plainly. Max Lucado, in his book *God Came Near*, notices something quite extraordinary in Jesus's response.

> But before the man said a word or heard a sound, Jesus did something I never would have anticipated. He sighed. I might have expected a clap or a song or a prayer. Even a "Hallelujah!" or a brief lesson might have been appropriate. But the Son of God did none of these. Instead, he paused, looked into heaven, and sighed. From the depths of His being came a rush of emotion that said more than words. Sigh. The word seemed out of place. I'd never thought of God as one who sighs. I'd thought of God as one who commands. I'd thought of God as one who called forth the dead with a command or created the universe with a word ... but a God who sighs? ... The apostle Paul spoke of this sighing. Twice he said that Christians will sigh as long as we are on earth and long for heaven. The creation sighs as if she were giving birth. Even the Spirit sighs as he interprets our prayers. ... And when Jesus looked into the eyes of Satan's victim, the only appropriate thing to do was sigh. "It was never intended to be this way," the sigh said. "Your ears weren't made to be deaf, your tongue wasn't made to stumble." The imbalance of it all caused the Master to languish. ... God's pain is our comfort. ... That holy sigh assures us that God still groans for His people. He groans for the day when all sighs will cease, when what was intended to be will be.[5]

God's patient love is shown as He sighs over His creation. "Not only so, but we ourselves, who have the first fruits of the Spirit, groan inwardly as we wait eagerly for our adoption as sons, the redemption of our bodies. ... But if we hope for what we do not yet have, we wait for it patiently" (Romans 8:23, 25 NIV).

Sometimes we wait patiently for what seems an eternity, and we wonder whether our dream will ever come to pass. What about the dream that is deferred—the dream that has dried up like a raisin in the sun? The dream that you have patiently waited for so long that never happens. After waiting for so long, do we give up on God? Or do we trust that He knows what is best for us? "For I know the plans I have for you," declares the Lord, "plans to prosper you and not to harm you, plans to give you a hope and a future" (Jeremiah 29:11 NIV). King David desired to build a house for God, but he never saw it. Yet his dream did not lie dormant in the grave, where so many dreams end up. God saw fit for David's son to build His house. Although David would never see God's house built, he worked diligently to provide the necessary building materials for the house and all its furnishings. Although we wait patiently, we should never give up on what God places in our hearts, and whatever we do, we must do it all for the glory of God, for He alone is worthy of all glory and honor.

14

Doing all things for the glory of God requires unselfish love, a love that puts others before ourselves.

In a farm family in which death took both parents in a short time, five children were left to make their own way. The eldest was a girl eighteen years of age who was determined to keep the orphan family together. On her rested responsibility of being both mother and father to younger ones. Work! Work! Work! She had to work from early morning until late at night: plowing, planting, harvesting, gardening, milking, canning, cooking, sewing, laundering and the doing of a hundred other things. In time, it broke her health; she developed tuberculosis where it finally reached its last stages. Realizing that life was gradually ebbing away, she said to the minister who often visited her, "I Know it won't be long until I reach the end and it seems I've done so little in life. I don't know what I'm going to tell the Lord for not doing more." The preacher said, "Don't tell Him anything. Just show Him your hands."[6]

Those were unselfish hands of a love so great that it completely forgot self. Unselfish love patiently gives and gives.

Jesus came not to be served but to serve. Rather than being called a servant, a better-known terminology for today is caregiving. One who must attend to another person's need is a caregiver. I was given the wonderful privilege of being my mother's caregiver for sixteen years. God began to prepare my heart months in advance for this task, as I was burdened with a need to take care of my mother. My parents were getting older, yet my father appeared to be healthier than my mother. One afternoon while at work, I received an emergency phone call from my mother telling me that she had rushed my father to the hospital for what appeared to be a sudden heart attack. Several weeks later, my father passed away due to an incorrectly diagnosed lung condition. After forty-six years of marriage, it seemed as though my mother would never smile again. I remember taking my mother home one day, and after seeing her into the house, I turned to walk away, and she called my name. I turned back around to see what she wanted, and I saw a smile on her face. She said, "Yonnie, you have my purse." Her smile sent waves of joy through my entire being.

I knew about the different steps of grieving, and I felt that time would heal things. In my mother's case, things continued to get worse rather than better. I began to look for other avenues of help. The path I was headed on began leading me to an area called dementia, a place that was totally foreign to me. I began reading whatever material that I could find on the subject. It was like piecing a puzzle together because every case was different.

Just as every person is different, there are also various types of dementia. My mother was given a test to see if she had dementia of the Alzheimer's type. Although she was diagnosed as such, I'm thankful to the Lord that my mother never went down that unknown path. She always knew who I was, as well as everyone who came to visit her.

It takes patience to be a caregiver, for they sometimes juggle many hats. While being a caregiver for my mother, I was also a wife, a mother of three, with the youngest still in elementary school, and a business owner. I must also mention that there are sixteen years between my oldest and my youngest child. My two older children were married and had children, which also made me a grandmother and a mother-in-law. As caregivers, we get tired and weary. But when much is given, much is required, and patience is at the top of the list.

In order to acquire patience, one must have an avenue of joy that stems from love. The Bible teaches that laughter is like good medicine. I remember being at my daughter's house one evening when a spirit of laughter came over me and I laughed so hard that I literally asked the Lord, "What is about to happen to me?" The next morning while I was at work, I called my mother as I usually did, but this particular morning, she didn't answer her phone. I tried calling several times, but still no answer. I cleared my desk at work, because for some strange reason I knew that I would not be returning that day. When I arrived at my mother's house, the screen door was thankfully unlocked, which it never was. I took my key, unlocked the storm door, and let myself in, only to find my mother on the floor, unable to get up. I called 911, and she was taken to the hospital, where I was told that she had the flu and was going to be admitted. After a week in the hospital, she was discharged but was told that she could not return to her home, so I brought her to my house even though I had to go to work every day. This move ushered me into a new season of patience.

When we experience new seasons in life, we are met with unforeseen issues. Dealing with my own patience was one thing, but now I found myself praying that others would be patient and kind. Although patience can be exemplified, it cannot be passed on one to another. In the case of dementia, the demented person may show characteristics that are sometimes strange and unexplainable. This type of behavior must be encountered with an abundance of love and kindness, which is the requirement of patience. If I had to do it all over again, I would love more and stress less. This is the true meaning of patient love.

God demonstrated to humankind the greatest action of patient love ever shown.

"For God so loved the world that He gave His only begotten Son" (John 3:16 KJV).

CHAPTER 2

LONG-SUFFERING

THE GREEK WORD FOR LONG-SUFFERING is *hypomone*, and it means to persevere in difficult circumstances. Long-suffering is the ability to bear trials without murmuring. You have heard of the patience of Job, how he was stripped of everything he owned, even his good health. "Then Job arose, tore his robe, and shaved his head; and he fell down to the ground, and worshiped. And he said, 'Naked I came from my mother's womb, and naked shall I return there. The Lord gave, and the Lord has taken away; Blessed be the name of the Lord.' In all this Job did not sin nor charge God with wrong" (Job 1:20-21 NKJV). Through his patience, Job was later blessed twofold over all he had lost.

So how does one obtain the sort of patience that Job possessed? When Job lost everything and His own wife encouraged him to "curse God and die" (Job 2:9 NKJV), he said, "Though He slay me, yet will I trust in Him" (Job 13:15 NKJV). Job could have become bitter over his circumstance, but instead, Job trusted God and kept his integrity: "I will maintain mine own ways before Him" (Job 13:15 KJV). Job refused to allow a devastating situation to change his God-given character, for he knew where his strength came from. "The Lord God is my strength" (Habakkuk 3:19 KJV). When we truly know that our strength comes from the Lord, we will not succumb to the ways of the world.

We in America have much to be thankful and grateful for. Yet we see suffering all around. Church massacres, school shootings, segregation, domestic violence, sickness, and the list goes on. Through whatever suffering we experience, God wants the glory. Nothing ever happens to us that God does not allow. Our suffering molds us into the likeness of God's Son. "For we do not have a high priest who is unable to sympathize with our weaknesses, but we have one who has been tempted in every way, just as we are—yet was without sin" (Hebrews 4:15 NIV). No matter how bad the situation may seem, God not only sympathizes with us, but He stands firmly beside us.

When we willingly suffer for the cause of Christ, the world will see that there is more to serving God than just lip service; they will see that we serve a God who is worthy of all our praise, in the good times as well as the bad times. A message will be sent to the world that God is a great God and all glory belongs to Him.

Some lessons of life are only learned through the school of suffering. God disciplines us through suffering, and through suffering we learn obedience. We learn to do what we are told, when we are told, with a happy heart. Through suffering, we learn compassion. We learn to be sensitive toward the suffering of others based on sound judgment. Through suffering, we learn empathy. We learn to understand the suffering of others. Through suffering, we learn lessons that grow our faith. And one of life's greatest lessons we learn is that when God wants to make a person great, He takes that person and crushes them. "But He said to me, 'My grace is sufficient for you, for my power is made perfect in weakness.' Therefore I will boast all the more gladly about my weakness, so that Christ's power may rest on me. That is why, for Christ's sake, I delight in weaknesses, in insults, in hardships, in persecutions, in difficulties. For when I am weak, then I am strong" (2 Corinthians 12:9-10 NIV). When we go through trials, our faith is tried, and patience is developed.

When we ask Christ into our hearts, we join God's army—an army that fights the good fight of faith. Yet some only join the army reserves and become weekend warriors. To be used fully by God, we must be all in for Christ. "For me to live is Christ, and to die is gain" (Philippians 1:21 KJV). Persecution may have harmful effects, causing some to become bitter and hateful. But on the other hand, suffering will cause some people to pray more and draw closer to Christ. He wants our hearts to be after Him and not after this world. "As the deer pants for the water brooks, so pants my soul for You, O God. My soul thirst for God, for the living God" (Psalm 42:1-2 NKJV). Suffering physically or emotionally for the cause of Christ demonstrates to the world that Jesus is more precious than anything the world has to offer. "The kingdom of heaven is like treasure hidden in a field, which a man found and hid; and for joy over it he goes and sells all that he has and buys that field" (Matthew 13:44 NKJV). More than worship or prayer, gladly accepting loss and suffering shows forth God's worth. Our joy in suffering will prove to the world that our treasure is in heaven and not on earth.

The stories of persecuted missionaries who suffered gladly for Christ have made God real and precious to many. "If anyone would come after me, let him deny himself and take up his cross and follow me" (Mark 8:34 NIV). The cross meets us at the beginning of our relationship with Christ. Christians who were martyred pursued love, not death. The call to suffer with Christ is not a call to bear our sins the way Jesus bore them but to love the way He loved. "I have been crucified with Christ. It is no longer I who live, but Christ who lives in me. And the life I now live in the flesh I live by faith in the Son of God, who loved me and gave himself for me" (Galatians 2:20 NKJV).

In the spring of 2018, I journeyed to Beijing, China, where I discovered that Christianity is not tolerated. President Xi Jimping came into power in 2012 and made himself president for life. At places of worship, crosses have been swapped for Chinese flags, reminding the citizens to prioritize the atheist Communist Party above all else or be subjected to reeducation programs. In China, there is the three-self church, a national political organization. The government formed the Three-Self Patriotic Church, which stands for self-propagating, self-supporting, and self-governing. The government created the Three-Self Patriotic Movement and allowed open, legal churches in order to control Christians and to promote their own political agenda inside the churches. The Christians in the three-self church are as birds confined in a cage, which also makes reproduction very hard.

The government and the three-self church have fooled many Christians around the world by insisting that Christians are no longer persecuted for their faith. Having a church building doesn't always mean that Jesus is with you. "Behold, I stand at the door and knock. If anyone hears My voice and opens the door, I will come in to him and dine with him, and he with Me" (Revelations 3:20 NKJV). We often hear this verse as inviting others to Christ, but in this verse, Jesus is standing outside the door of the church in Laodicea, knocking to get in. In the three-self church, the caged birds with the clipped wings are not the problem, the government is. Within the three-self church, the government does not allow ministry without permission. Evangelism is discouraged. All outreach to children is strictly banned. It is decreed that certain parts of the Bible cannot be preached, such as the Second Coming of the Lord Jesus. They are not allowed to teach on divine healing or the deliverance of demons. The entire book of Revelation is banned.

The true church is not organized and controlled by the rules of humans but has Jesus Christ as the cornerstone. The Chinese government cannot stand the free birds who refuse to come under its control. The government hunts down and traps the free birds and cages them behind iron bars. Yet, even behind bars, the free birds lay eggs and multiply, winning souls to the Lord in prison.

Brother Yun, one of China's house church leaders, suffered prolonged torture and imprisonment for his faith. After multiple beatings and tortures, Brother Yun's legs were so severely broken and smashed that he could no longer walk. While lying in horrendous pain, Brother Yun had a vision and felt that the Lord was giving him his hour of salvation. In his book *The Heavenly Man*, Brother Yun and Hattaway, share Brother Yun's miraculous prison escape; it's as if one were hearing Peter's escape in Acts 12:5-11.

It all happened on May 5, 1997, just before eight o'clock in the morning. Brother Yun experienced being freed from prison the same way Peter did, as described in Acts 12:5-19. As he walked past the guards, they looked straight through him as though he was invisible. Every gate that he came to was open, and even the main gate to the prison stood ajar. With Yun's heart pounding, he found himself standing on the street outside the Zhengzhou Number One Maximum Security Prison. A taxi driver pulled up and asked him where he was headed. Brother Yun found out later that no one had ever escaped from this prison before.

"Just as it is written: 'God has given them a spirit of stupor, eyes that they should not see and ears that they should not hear, to this very day'" (Romans 11:8 NKJV). Nothing happens to us or for us without God allowing it. "Beloved, do not think it strange concerning the fiery trial which is to try you, as though some strange thing happened unto you; but rejoice to the extent that you partake of Christ's sufferings, that when His glory is revealed, you may also be glad with exceeding joy. If you are reproached for the name of Christ, blessed are you, for the Spirit of glory and of God rests upon you. On their part He is blasphemed, but on your part, He is glorified" (1 Peter 4:12-14 NKJV).

Brother Yun's testimony is written with blood and tears. Instead of complaining and grumbling, he learned to tackle all obstacles prayerfully, on his knees patiently with God.

> They separated my fingers and held them palm-
> down on a wooden board. The doctor took a
> large needle, labelled number 6, from his bag.
> He jabbed the needle and I can't describe how I
> felt. It was the most excruciating agony I've ever
> experienced. Intense pain shot through my entire
> body. I couldn't help but cry out ... Thank God He
> protected and preserved me through these trials. I
> knew that God was using the wrath of evil men to
> accomplish His purpose in me, to break down my
> self-centeredness and my stubbornness. He taught
> me how to wait on Him, how to patiently endure
> hardship, and how to love the family of God in a
> more real way.[7]

From January 25 until April 7 in 1984, while Brother Yun was in prison for the sake of the Gospel, Yun did not eat any food or drink any water for seventy-four days. His weight dropped to sixty pounds, and much of his hair fell out from being beaten and kicked. His ears shriveled to the size of raisins. His whole appearance had changed because of the electric shock therapy that prison guards had used on him. He was unrecognizable by his own wife. His mother knew him to be her son only by his birthmark. As a humble servant of God, Yun desires that his testimony will focus all attention and glory on the Lord Jesus Christ. "Rejoice in hope of the glory of God. And not only so, but we glory in tribulations also: knowing that tribulation worketh patience" (Romans 5:3-4 KJV). We suffer long that Christ may be glorified. Brother Yun found that suffering is part of the struggle for the name of Christ. "If you are insulted because of the name of Christ, you are blessed, for the Spirit of glory and of God rests on you" (1 Peter 4:14 NIV).

To be partakers of Christ's suffering, we must be prepared to stamp out our personal ambitions. We must prepare for God to destroy our individual decisions by supernatural transformation. Within this transformation, we will not know where God is taking us, for knowing God's plan afore time will make us spiritually proud. We will not understand the reason for what God is putting us through, until suddenly we come to a place of enlightenment and realize that God has strengthened us and we didn't even know it.

"But whoever slaps you on your right cheek, turn the other to him also" (Matthew 5:39 NKJV). Only those who have suffered long are qualified to turn the other cheek. The spirit of patience is a quality that is developed. Patience is not cowardice, for it requires courage to be patient. We are strong only because God is strong in us. In order to develop patience, we must go through some things, but we must not forget where our help comes from. Our help comes from the Lord who made heaven and earth. Only the patient who have suffered injury are prepared to obey this command: "Love your enemies, bless them that curse you, do good to them that hate you, and pray for them which despitefully use you, and persecute you" (Matthew 5:44 KJV).

CHAPTER 3

WHERE PATIENCE
IS FOUND

"BUT THEY THAT WAIT UPON the Lord shall renew their strength; they shall mount up with wings as eagles; they shall run, and not be weary; and they shall walk, and not faint" (Isaiah 40:31 KJV). We will never be satisfied with earthbound existence; our spirits were made to soar. "Behold the fowls of the air" (Matthew 6:26 KJV). The captive-born, imprisoned eagle feels the instinct to fly but does not know what it longs for. Our spirits were made to fly away from whatever hampers or imprisons us here. Our spirits were made to fly away to a place where patience is found.

As a young mother, while visiting my grandmother one day, I discovered a book that was housed among the many other books on her living room bookshelf. It totally captivated my spiritual thinking and changed my life, leaving me with a hunger and a desire to learn more of God's truths. I will be forever grateful for Hannah Whitall Smith and Catherine Jackson, who paraphrased *The Christian's Secret of a Happy Life for Today.*

This book spoke to my restlessness and discontented spirit while I was searching for a way to escape my outward circumstances. I hadn't realized that my only way to escape was to mount up with wings when I was trying so very hard to "flee upon horses" (Isaiah 30:16 KJV), just as the Israelites had done before the fall of Jerusalem. Our "horses" are the worldly ways of escape: entertainment, human companionship, travel, a new job, a new marriage. We mount on these and run off in all directions, desiring to get away from our trouble—only to learn that patience is not found in any of these distractions that tend to disturb our souls. The spirit is not made to flee on horses; it must always fly on wings.

So, what are these spiritual wings? *They who wait on the Lord.* To wait on God is to be entirely surrendered to Him, to trust Him perfectly. Therefore, our wings are surrender and trust. The Christian who learns the secrets of absolute surrender and perfect trust will be able to mount up on these wings and take flight to "heavenly places in Christ" (Ephesians 1:3 KJV), where one's life is hid with Christ in God, where no earthly annoyance or sorrow has the power to disturb them. It is completely independent of circumstances; it is the place where patience is found. No cage can imprison, and no shackles can bind the believer whose wings have carried them to this height.

The view of life from the patient place is totally different from that of the Christian whose mind is fixed on things here on earth. The caterpillar crawling on the ground has a very limited view of its surroundings. Yet how different the world appears to that same caterpillar after it develops butterfly wings and soars above the places where it once crawled.

We rise on wings of surrender and trust, into the upper territories of the patient life that is in Christ, where a believer becomes "more than a conqueror" (Romans 8:37 KJV). A "life that is hid in Christ" (Colossians 3:3 KJV) is a life that is lived on wings. "Oh that I had the wings of a dove! I would fly away and be at rest. I would flee far away and stay in the desert; I would hurry to my place of shelter, far from the tempest and storm" (Psalm 55:6–8 NIV). A life that is hid in Christ is where patience is found.

I recall, when growing up, my pastor often saying that a person is either coming out of a storm, in a storm, or going into a storm. We run from one trouble to another. Amos 5:19 (NIV) puts it this way: "It will be as though a man fled from a lion only to meet a bear, as though he entered his house and rested his hand on the wall only to have a snake bite him." We cannot avoid trouble, nor can we escape trouble by running to an earthly refuge. Through patience, we come to know that the Lord is our refuge and strong tower. Therefore, "I will lift mine eyes to the hills, from whence cometh my help. My help cometh from the Lord, which made heaven and earth" (Psalm 121:1-2 KJV). When we patiently use our spiritual wings, we can escape the things that threaten to harm us. The earthly plane may look dark, but in the heavenly plane of patience, there will be sunshine. In the patient palace, "I will rejoice in the Lord, I will joy in the God of my salvation" (Habakkuk 3:18 KJV).

The church would be different if Christians would learn how to use their wings of surrender and trust when coping with problems that concern human relationships. If sisters and brothers in Christ would patiently trust God to deal with offenses, they would find themselves mounting up on wings. Instead of returning evil for evil and stirring up strife and contention, problems would be solved with the patient love and compassion of Christ. And if the love that we give to our enemy does not remove the animosity from their heart, we have become better for trying. The more we patiently love, the more we are changed into the likeness of God.

God created our spirits to live in the upper atmosphere; therefore, He plans our lives so that we will have plenty of opportunities for flying lessons. "As an eagle stirs up its nest, hovers over its young, spreading out its wings, taking them up, carrying them on its wings, so the Lord alone led him, and there was no foreign god with him. He made him ride in the heights of the earth" (Deuteronomy 32:11-13 NKJV). A mother bird stirs up the nest, making it uncomfortable so that her babies will be forced to leave and learn to fly. That's what God does for His children. He patiently allows for life to become uncomfortable. Then He pushes us over the edge so that we are forced to use our wings in order to try to save ourselves, and in the process, we learn how to fly.

When we look at our problems in this light and thankfully accept our situations, our wings are forced to grow strong enough to carry us to the patient "heavenly places in Christ" (Ephesians 1:3 KJV). And as it is with any muscle, if you don't use patience, you will lose it. Using our patient wing muscles prevents losing all capacity to fly. Have you ever seen someone lose their patience and fly off the handle? They have flown into restricted territory. They have flown outside of the patient place, where turbulence resides. This turbulence can lead to stress, which is a cause of illness that includes high blood pressure, heart attack, stroke, and mental illness.

A bird may try to use their strong wings, but conditions have made flight impossible. Perhaps the bird may be caged, or tied with a cord to the ground, or entrapped in the "snare of the fowler" (Psalm 91:3 KJV). Similarly, a Christian may be snared to such things as a lack of consecration, where one has not surrendered to God, and thereby their patient wings are disabled. Another snare is doubt, which is totally disabling, for it is just like having a broken wing. As long as the patient wing of trust is caught in the snare of doubt, one can never rise above the earth circumstances and experience heavenly patience.

Sometimes one may feel as though their spirit is in an inescapable prison, where even with wings, an upward flight is hindered. "But your iniquities have separated you from your God" (Isaiah 59:2 NKJV). Unless you renounce and confess sin that has separated you from God, you will not be able to fly. If we allow worldly concerns and anxieties to weigh us down or tether our spirit to the earth and keep us from flying, our souls will be unable to rise any higher than an eagle that is bolted to the ground. We likely have all lost our patience at some point. But when this happens frequently or inappropriately, this can harm our reputation, damage relationships, increase stress, and intensify a difficult situation. "Let us lay aside every weight, and the sin which does so easily beset us, and let us run with patience the race that is set before us" (Hebrews 12:1 KJV).

On a trip to Mongolia in 2018, I had an opportunity to hold an eagle. It's weight and the strong clench of its claws clamping around my wrist was almost startling. But even more surprising was the eagle's amazing six-foot wingspan. Yet even the largest wings cannot lift an eagle one inch off the ground unless they are used. It is the same with Christians; their spiritual wings must be used if they are to experience patience.

Every human soul has two wings; one is called surrender, and the other is called trust. A Christian does not need more wings, but what is needed is the courage to use the power to surrender and trust. When we use these two wings, we can mount up to God at any moment and find patience—but only if we use them. Having a desire to use them is not enough; we must actively do so. A notional surrender of patience or an occasional moment of patient trust is ineffective. We must patiently surrender to God each detail of our daily lives as it comes to us and patiently trust God to work together all things for our good. We must surrender to God the trivial hassles in life, the petty frustrations that are beyond our control, things like getting stuck in traffic or waiting for a computer program to load. Having the ability to surrender to God these mundane matters is a show of faith, and one becomes more empathetic and reasonable.

Two wings are needed to lift a bird above the earth. If you have ever watched a bird try to fly with a broken wing, you have seen how ineffective one-sided flying can be. Just as a bird needs two wings to fly, so it is with a Christian; the wings of surrender and trust are both needed. No matter how we use the wing of surrender, if the wing of trust is caught in the snare of doubt, we will never rise far from the earth.

We must patiently meet our trials and temptations of every sort with an attitude of active and practical surrender and trust. Only then will we be able to spread our wings and fly above them all to the heavenly places in Christ, where patience is found. From this patient vantage point, we will be able to see our problems through the eyes of Jesus, and the things that so easily beset us will lose their power to harm or distress us.

CHAPTER 4

A PATIENT SPIRIT IS
SLOW TO ANGER

"BE ANGRY AND SIN NOT" (Ephesians 4:26 KJV). We must not allow anger to control us. Moments of anger may be experienced in small annoyances or overwhelming circumstances. When we lash out at someone with harsh words, we find ourselves feeling guilty or ashamed. Yet still there are times when anger is not wrong, and we call this righteous anger. This is the time when sin is attacked, not the sinner. God hates sin and is offended by its very nature, yet He loves the sinner. Therefore, we must ask ourselves questions such as, Is our anger intended to make the world better in a loving way? Does our anger draw others to Christ? Or does our anger cause another to lose heart in their faith and draw away from Christ? God looks at the intentions of the heart. However, when we get angry, we must patiently consider how we respond to others. For example, becoming angry if we saw someone mistreating an animal would be all right. On the other hand, it would not be all right for someone to become angry, then take a gun and shoot the person responsible for mistreating the animal. In the book of John, Jesus made a whip from some ropes and drove the people out of the temple. This action of Jesus was done out of righteous indignation. God is holy and must be treated as holy. The temple represented God's house, and when Jesus saw that His Father's house had been turned into a marketplace, He was consumed with righteous anger.

Even though Jesus broke down the middle wall of hostility by dying on the cross so that we could have peace, people still get angry. So how does a person relieve themselves of anger? Should they scream, punch a bag, tear up a newspaper, or vent to a friend? Or is it more effective to walk away and count to ten? We can try to come up with ways to relieve anger, but the fact remains that unrighteous anger is a sin issue. Sin is deceptive and can distort our ability to think reasonably and rationally. Through God's patient love, we have been made alive by Christ's death, burial, and resurrection. Because of Jesus, we are able to pursue humility and meekness. Meekness is strength under control that resembles a well-trained warrior.

Patience is a fruit of the Spirit, and those who obtain patience are ruled by the Spirit. If we are going to refrain from outbursts of hurtful anger, we must be filled with the Spirit. Before we can be filled with the Spirit, we must be set free, and it is Jesus who sets us free. Anger can lead one to sin because the intemperate are not free; they are enslaved to cruel bondage, servants to sin. When we make Jesus our master, we are no longer a servant to sin. We do not have to succumb to anger; we are free to live a Spirit-filled life.

There are times when people seem as though they want to try our patience. They offend us over and over, and we find ourselves crying out to God for Him to keep us in perfect peace. When our patience is tried, we must not give in or give up. In the book of Genesis, we find Isaac staying in Gerar, where the Lord blessed him and he became very rich. The Philistines envied Isaac for his wealth, which caused Abimelech the king to tell Isaac that he must leave. Isaac left Gerar and built a well, but out of jealousy, the people of Gerar filled it up. Isaac moved and built another well, and once again, they covered it up. Isaac moved and built another well for the third time, and this time the well remained uncovered. Isaac's patience was exemplified, and Abimelech saw that the Lord was with Isaac. When we demonstrate patience, God is glorified. There is nothing about impatience that gives God glory. If our desire is for God to be exalted, we must show a spirit of patience.

A person of understanding realizes that patience wards off anger by blocking the enemy, who would like to intercede and capture our peace. But God will not have us ignorant concerning the schemes of the enemy. When we patiently take the time to listen to God, we will hear the Holy Spirit speaking peace to our hearts, because God is not the author of confusion. The righteousness of God cannot be produced by the anger of humans. If you constantly think angry thoughts, you will become an angry person. For what you think in your heart, you will become. We must ask God to create in us a clean heart so that the meditation of our hearts will be acceptable to God.

Peace is not the absence of turmoil but the realization that when the waters of life are raging, we understand that it is God who created the water. No one desires to have storms in their life, but storms of life are inevitable. One is either coming out of a storm, in a storm, or headed to a storm. Therefore, peace is not the absence of storms but the presence of God in the midst of the storm.

What we learn about peace comes through patience. In our patience, we will hear God tell us, "Be still and know that I am

God!" Patience will allow us to experience God's assurance of calm, the peace that surpasses all knowledge. We must be patient with others, and we must also be patient with ourselves. When we become angry with ourselves and this anger is not dealt with, it will turn inward and result in depression. There are times when we must forgive ourselves. Perhaps one has made a wrong decision or no decision at all, and they have become indecisive. Yet there are times when we do not have a clue as to why we are depressed. We ask ourselves why we are so down, only to discover that we have no answer. At times like these, we must patiently trust in God, for He knows our hearts' deepest thoughts, and He is able to deliver us from ourselves.

Anger can be found in any personality and temperament. Anger can be found in a shy person or an extrovert, a perfectionist or one who is laid back. The reaction to anger can be expressed in many ways. Anger may be shown through frustration, fussing, touchiness, aggravation, or blowing off steam. Anger may also come in different forms: explosive, silent, or irritable. It can hurt those whom we are called to love the most. Although God can become angry, His anger is never sinful, and He is always slow to anger. God's wrath for all our sins culminated onto Jesus when He went to the cross to pay the penalty for our sin. No matter what we have said with our mouth, or done physically to harm others or ourselves, we can be forgiven and walk in the newness of life. We can be set free from a vicious cycle of anger by humbly stepping down from our judgment seat and allowing God to be God as we surrender our sinful anger to Him. The cycle of anger will be broken only when one has made a conscious choice. God is patient and will give grace in the time of need.

The way in which we respond to anger, whether good or bad, is a choice. When someone is constantly getting angry, a pattern is being repeated, and the only way to break the anger cycle is to make a conscious choice to manage the anger.

When someone triggers us and makes us angry, we must not look at the other person and blame them; we must look at ourselves. Our anger was triggered by something that was already in us. Our anger is a reflection, a mirror of us. We are the source of our anger because the issues of life flow out of the heart. When painful circumstances trigger an angry response within us, we can choose to respond in a way that is unhealthy or in a way that is healthy.

One unhealthy way to respond to anger is suppressing it. Suppressed anger may come in the form of denial or fronting an image of not being rattled. Suppressed anger represents a feeling of personal defeat. One may feel that there is no need to express angry feelings, because they have reached a point where they feel as though they do not matter, or their feelings do not matter, or both; this is a feeling of worthlessness. Then there are others who suppress anger out of fear of what they may do or who they may hurt.

A second unhealthy response to anger is open aggression, which is what most people think of when they think of anger. Open aggression comes in the form of explosive rage, shouting, intimidation, blame, criticism, and sarcasm. This expression of anger is at the expense of someone else. It is self-centered and comes off as not caring at all about the other person. Because of deep insecurities, some people try to make themselves larger in an effort to make themselves heard.

Still another form of unhealthy anger is passive aggression, which is displayed through a strong competitive spirit when there is a need to control. Passive aggression uses subtle sabotage through dishonesty and slyness. People who display passive aggression do not want to get caught being angry because they believe that the expression of anger is sinful or disgraceful.

To manage anger in a healthy and responsible way, one must have a reasonable issue and communicate in a caring and rational manner. There are times when one must express anger assertively.

Assertive anger does not mean being pushy or abrasive; nor is it meant to harm. While considering the needs and feelings of others, we express anger to preserve our self-worth, needs, and convictions. When we express our anger assertively rather than aggressively, we enable our relationships to grow stronger as we demonstrate maturity and stability. Assertiveness is not always easy because it requires self-discipline and respect for the dignity of others. The assertive approach says that I matter and you matter too, and we don't have the right to hurt each other. Anger can have a healthful, self-sustaining function in our lives if approached fairly and directly. Being assertive is a caring, healthy, helpful, and effectual way to handle anger.

The healthiest way to express anger is to drop it. Although dropping anger is healthy, it is the most difficult way to express anger. Dropping anger means you accept your inability to control circumstances, and you recognize your personal limits. Choosing to drop anger includes tolerating differences and choosing to forgive. Dropping anger is different from suppressing anger because suppression represents phoniness and denial. Dropping anger shows a commitment to live a life uncluttered by bitterness and discord. Choosing to drop anger represents a commitment to godliness. Grudges are an option, but when we drop anger, we choose to remove bitterness and discord from our lives. Our emotional response must be chosen today, by living in the now. We must choose to forgive today and not worry about forgiving tomorrow. Dropping anger is a form of forgiveness, and although you forgave yesterday, forgiveness may be required once again today. When we learn new information about a misdeed and old frustrations well up inside, causing anger, it may be difficult to forgive once and for all, yet we must continue to forgive the same offense over and over whenever it comes to mind, until eventually it fades away. Forgiveness is an act of the will, which means we must make a choice that is totally up to us. Forgiveness is a healthy action of self-love.

Forgiveness does not mean reconciliation, because it takes two to reconcile. When an abuser is not willing to change, reconciliation can be harmful. In order to live a healthy life and please God, there may be times when one has to remove both the abuser and bitterness.

Another type of anger is called displaced anger. For example, one might experience anger with a supervisor but instead direct it to a spouse. Unfortunately, this type of anger may sometimes be rooted in past history that triggers some form of childhood event that yields anger. No matter where the anger stems from, we are not hopeless. God is more than able to deliver us from all situations if we patiently trust Him to do so and believe that He is able. If we are not patient and our hope is only in instant gratification, we must stop and realize that God works in His time frame and not ours. God knows what it takes to get us to where He wants us to be. God orchestrates the ways we take, but we must patiently trust in Him to do so.

The sooner we deal with anger issues, the better. Anger that is not dealt with can become poisonous and turn a heart bitter. A bitter person is a hurting person, and a hurting person will hurt others. A bitter person will hurt the very ones they love the most. Love is meant to be patient with others, for it is love that covers a multitude of sins.

King David committed adultery, and the woman was found to be with child. To cover up his sin, David had the woman's husband murdered. Nathan the prophet came to David and told him a story about a poor man who had only one little lamb, which he cherished. A rich man came along and cooked the poor man's little lamb for dinner so that he could serve it to his guest. Upon hearing this news, David became very angry and wanted the rich man killed. Nathan told David that he was the man, and he went on to tell David everything he had done. David was brokenhearted, his spirit was crushed, and he became very sorry. Immediately, David repented and asked God to forgive him.

When it comes to anger, we must consider our ways. We must always accept responsibility and never blame others for our actions. When we accept responsibility for actions that surround our anger, repentance must follow. Repentance is being sorry for your actions and asking for forgiveness. True repentance, however, goes a step further by changing one's mind concerning the actions. This is accomplished by turning from the old way of acting and turning to a new and better way. Patiently considering our ways, will help us to refrain from sinning and prevent a lot of heartache and misery.

Whatever way we express anger, it is a result of the choice we make. There is a time when anger has a place, and there is a time when we must drop anger. It is inappropriate to express anger at the expense of someone else by using means of sarcasm, shouting, criticizing, blaming, intimidating, or acts of explosive rage. This act of open aggression is self-centered anger, and it degrades the other person, making them feel as though they and their feelings don't matter.

Anger thrives on unmet needs, and when those needs are not met, we experience anger. Humans need love, and when we constantly feel loved, our emotions will be displayed through stability. When love is lacking, the response to rejected feelings will be anger. When people feel rejected, left out, ignored, or misunderstood, they become angry. The more a person struggles with anger, the more it indicates their love tank has gone unfulfilled, either in adulthood or childhood. Long-stored anger will turn into resentment and depression.

One may feel a need to be in control, yet when one feels controlled by another, anger arises. We do need structure and organization to maintain peace in our lives; therefore, control is not always bad. We find that anger arises when a controlling person eliminates choices for another person, erasing any chance of them making a mistake or action of irresponsibility. At this point, control becomes excessive, and one begins to feel as though they are not trusted by the controlee. The person being controlled does not have to subject themselves to the abuse or controlling behavior of another. A choice can be made to state their position by verbalizing their angry feelings as they speak the truth in love, gently, respectfully, and tactfully. After stating one's opinion, a choice to move on can be made through humility rather than self-preoccupied pride. Anger that is expressed in a self-controlled and loving way, with the goal of making constructive changes in a relationship, is a powerful force for healing.

While being slow to speak, we must patiently evaluate our anger. Whatever comes out of our mouth, we cannot put back in. Our words must be spoken truthfully with love in order to bring about restoration and not revenge. When we verbalize our anger, we should not blame others, but we should own what we feel. This is done by using statements such as "I feel angry," rather than saying, "You made me angry." Owning what we feel allows us to choose forgiveness. As we identity our feelings, we must not dwell on them.

God does not want us to respond to life and all its challenges in a way that is natural to the flesh. Revenge is a natural response to the flesh, and God does not want this. He wants a supernatural response of forgiveness. Forgiveness is not fair, but it is the only way to be fair to ourselves. People who hurt us do not deserve forgiveness, but we deserve to forgive. It wasn't fair for God to place our sin on Jesus, nor was it fair for Jesus to die on the cross for our sin. But we are ever so grateful for God's love, grace, and mercy. Therefore, we do not deserve forgiveness; we deserve to forgive.

The book of Psalms tells us that we are shaped in iniquity. We see anger demonstrated in children through a display of temper tantrums when the children are upset or frustrated. Temper tantrums should be treated as opportunities for education as a child learns to deal with frustration over time. Temper tantrums are common during the second year of life. A toddler's inability to handle the desire for independency and control over their environment can turn into power struggles. As children mature and their language skills develop, they learn to cooperate, communicate, and deal with frustration as they gain self-control. When a child gains self-control through patience, there will be fewer temper tantrums and happier parents.

"Train up a child in the way that he should go" (Proverbs 22:6 KJV). A parent must respond patiently to a tantrum by helping the child to calm down, depending on why the child is upset. If a child is in need of comfort, maybe they are hungry or tired, and a snack or nap is needed. If the tantrum is to get a parent's attention, the best way to reduce this type of behavior is to ignore it. If a child has a tantrum because they were refused something, the parent must stay calm and move on to another activity. If the child refuses to do something they were told to do, ignore the tantrum but make sure the task is completed after the child has calmed down. After the child has regained control, the parent should let the child know that they like how they have calmed down. At this point, a hug should be given to reassure the child that they are loved no matter what.

Still, the best way to handle temper tantrums is to prevent them from happening with praise and attention. Offer minor choices in order to give the child some control over things. For example, "Do you want to take a bath before or after you brush your teeth?" Or, "Do you want apple juice or orange juice?" Objects that are off limits should be kept out of sight and out of reach. To replace something that is frustrating or forbidden, start a new activity or move to a different environment either inside or outside the house. Help children learn to do things, starting with small things, and then move up. Praise them in order to make them feel proud of what they can do. Consider a child's request carefully, thereby choosing your battles. Know your child's limits. Is it time for their nap before tackling one more errand?

We are God's children, and our Father knows what is best for us. God tenderly and patiently leads and guides because He knows the way we were created. God looks at us with eyes of love, for He knows that it was not meant to be this way, that we were not meant to live in anger. In the Garden of Eden, man disobeyed, and his eyes became open, knowing good and evil, and man came to know anger. Yet God did not leave us alone in our anger. He provided a way out. By God's mercy and grace, a way was provided for humankind to be reconciled back to the Father through His Son, Jesus. Through Jesus's death, burial, and resurrection, we have

been forgiven, and through Christ we are able to forgive ourselves
and others. When we accept Christ's forgiveness, we are no longer a
slave to anger; we have been set free—free to love and patiently free
to forgive one another. God patiently leads us and guides us in the
newness of life—a life that is not bound by anger.

CHAPTER 5

PATIENCE PRODUCES
PEACE

"BUT WHEN YOU DO GOOD and suffer, if you take it patiently, this is commendable before God" (1 Peter 2:20 NKJV). When Jesus was abused and insulted, He did not retaliate. When He suffered, He did not threaten to hurt back. Instead, He committed Himself to God.

Sometimes we suffer long, enduring circumstances that we or no other person has cause or control over. Despite Christ's compassionate death for our sins, God has a specific plan for all Christians to suffer. God does not say that into each life a little rain must fall and then aim a hose in earth's direction and see who gets the wettest. In God's wisdom and love, every trial in a Christian's life is ordained from eternity past and is especially made for that believer's eternal good, even when it does not seem like it. Nothing happens by accident, not even tragedy or sins committed against us. God teaches us to hate our sins, to grow up spiritually, and to love Him. He gives us the benefits of salvation gradually by allowing us to feel sin's sting while we are headed to heaven. Suffering is a constant reminder of the hell that we are being delivered from. Through suffering, we learn patience, and through patience, we obtain peace.

Joni Erickson Tada, at the age of seventeen, severed her spinal cord in a diving accident and became a quadriplegic. After fifty-three years, Joni still remains in her wheelchair. Joni, who has patiently suffered for so many years, shares her thoughts about suffering: "Suffering has no meaning in itself. Left to its own, it is a frustrating and bewildering burden. But given the context of relationship, suffering suddenly has meaning."[8] Reasons will reach the head, but it is our relationships that will reach our souls. Jesus is relational, for there is no suffering that we may go through that He is unable to sympathize with.

For those who have not arrived at this level of spiritual maturity, the question may still be, Why? Why do good people suffer bad things? Romans 3:10 (NKJV) tells us, "There is none righteous, no, not one." Is it self-righteous to think that one should not suffer? Or perhaps is suffering a way to give the world a glimpse of hell? For, if one thought of suffering as a place of divine punishment on earth, then perhaps one would draw near to God in order to prevent going to an eternal hell. One might ponder the next life if they had a taste of hell in this life. Suffering then may be looked upon as the roadblock that prevents our journey to hell, the detour that redirects eternity. If it were not for suffering, one might continue in their lifestyle of sin, never allowing themselves to ponder the consequences. But God in His kindness puts up a warning sign that says, "Stop! Danger Ahead!" This warning sign may come in the form of sickness, financial or marital troubles, or a wayward child. Whatever way God chooses, this warning sign is designed to get our undivided attention. When we view suffering as a way to get our attention, God is no longer seen as one who sits back and allows whatever to happen, but He is understood as a patient God who allows things to happen for our good.

Through life, we follow many twists and turns, but God says, "He knows the way that I take" (Job 23:10 NKJV). It may seem as though one is destined for hell, yet even through our foolishness, "God is longsuffering toward us, not willing that any should perish but that all should come to repentance" (2 Peter 3:9 NKJV). C. S.

Lewis said, "Sin is the human being saying to God throughout life, 'Go away and leave me alone.' Hell is God finally saying to the human, 'You may have your wish.' It is God leaving the person to himself or herself, as that individual has chosen."[9] Joni says, "Human suffering in this life is merely the splash over from hell. God's plan for us in this life is to give us the benefits of heaven only gradually. By letting us struggle with remnants of a sinful nature, and by letting us know pain, he reminds us of the hell we are being saved from."[10] The fact that God does not leave us alone by allowing suffering is a reminder that God does not want us to go to hell.

When we cannot find the strength to live the life that God has issued us, we must call on God for help. "My grace is sufficient for you, for My strength is made perfect in weakness" (2 Corinthians 12:9 NKJV). What we cannot do, God can. When we humbly go to God and say, "Help me," God will move mountains for us if we get out of the way and allow Him to do so. Trusting in God and not ourselves is a process that is learned over time. When we look back and recall how God did it before, then surely we can trust Him to do it again. Drawing near to God is the magnetic force of faith. "Draw near to God and He will draw near to you" (James 4:8 NKJV). "God always seems bigger to those who need him the most. And suffering is the tool he uses to help us need him more."[11] A mother of ten children was once asked the question, "Which child do you love the most?" The mother responded by saying, "The child who needs me most." "The Lord is close to the brokenhearted and saves those who are crushed in spirit" (Psalm 34:18 NIV).

Long-suffering teaches us that God is more concerned with character than comfort. "Not only so, but we also glory in our sufferings, because we know that suffering produces perseverance; perseverance, character; and character, hope" (Romans 5:3-4 NIV). There are some things in life that only pain can change. Long-suffering teaches us that the greatest good of the Christian life is not absence of pain but Christlikeness. "We are hard pressed on every side, but not crushed; perplexed, but not in despair; persecuted, but not abandoned; struck down, but not destroyed. We always carry around in our body the death of Jesus, so that the life of Jesus may also be revealed in our body" (2 Corinthians 4:8-10 NIV).

Jesus always saves and sanctifies through suffering. When we come to the realization that there is absolutely nothing we can do to change our situation, we realize that suffering bankrupts us, making us dependent on God. "My grace is sufficient for you, for my power is made perfect in weakness. Therefore I will boast all the more gladly about my weaknesses, so that Christ's power may rest on me" (2 Corinthians 12:9 NIV).

God grant me the serenity to accept
the things I cannot change;
courage to change the things I can;
and wisdom to know the difference.[12]
—Reinhold Nicbuhr

We must study God's Word until we know what is right, and then we must stand by our confession through the good and the bad. It is one thing to hold on to God's promises in good times, but it is when we find ourselves all alone on the battlefield of life that we must learn to hold on to our belief and confess what we believe, or else we will speak life one day to our situations and death the next. "Let us hold fast the profession of our faith without wavering; for He is faithful that promised" (Hebrews 10:23 KJV). Our profession of faith is whatever God has promised us. We must believe God, and then we must keep believing until we see it. The Word, which is truth, makes us free only when we embrace truth and become truth ourselves. "If you continue in My Word, then are ye My disciples indeed; and ye shall know the truth, and the truth shall make you free" (John 8:31-32 KJV). As we patiently study and believe God's Word, we must hold on to God's promises.

When our thinking is lined up with the Word of God, we will not be swayed by the world. "For as he thinks in his heart, so is he" (Proverbs 23:7 NKJV). We cannot say one thing and believe another. "Everything in your life depends on what you think, and this is because what you think is what you say, and what you say is what you get."[13] Our thinking becomes right when we know and understand the goodness of God, and it is then that we will begin to talk and act right.

The Word of God never changes, so our confession should never change no matter what comes our way. The woman with the issue of blood for twelve long years did not give up hope. She said, "If I may but touch his garment, I shall be whole" (Matthew 9:21 KJV). She pressed her way through and was made whole. No matter what comes our way, we must stand on God's Word. We have to press through, whether it be good or bad. "Wherefore take unto you the whole armor of God, that you may be able to withstand in the evil day, and having done all, to stand" (Ephesians 6:13 KJV). Just stand! Whatever our particular situation is, know that we will be victorious as we persevere in faith and hold fast our confession to the glory of God. He does not want us to be double-minded or wishy-washy like a wave tossed back and forth.

"Do you not know that in a race all the runners run, but only one gets the prize? Run in such a way as to get the prize. Everyone who competes in the game goes into strict training. They do it to get a crown that will not last, but we do it to get a crown that will last forever. Therefore I do not run like someone running aimlessly; I do not fight like a boxer beating the air. No, I strike a blow to my body and make it my slave so that after I have preached to others, I myself will not be disqualified for the prize" (1 Corinthians 9:24-27 NIV).

We patiently hold on to God's Word because His Word is righteous, and righteous thoughts lead to righteous actions. "Finally, brethren, whatsoever things are true, whatsoever things are honest, whatsoever things are just, whatsoever things are pure, whatsoever things are lovely, whatsoever things are of good report; if there be any virtue, and if there be any praise, think on these things" (Philippians 4:8 KJV). God does not want us to dwell on negativity, nor does He want us to think on things that are not Christlike. We are not to think on things that will so easily beset us. God tells us not to dwell on things that bring about doubt and fear. When we are patient, we will ponder our thoughts, not desiring for wrong thoughts to creep in. We are to avoid things that will turn our hearts and minds away from God. Patience will be produced by giving purposeful, gentle, and slow thought to a matter or situation.

The things that wrongly affect us do not jump out with detouring red flags; instead, they subtly sneak through the cracks. These subtle things may come in forms that are wrapped up in movies and sometimes songs that at first seem OK and harmless as innocent doves, but they are shrewd as snakes that attach themselves to our minds, and like sponges, they soak the mind with the very things that God hates. "These six things the Lord hates, yes, seven are an abomination to Him: A proud look, a lying tongue, hands that shed innocent blood, a heart that devises wicked plans, feet that are swift in running to evil, a false witness who speaks lies, and one who sows discord among brethren" (Proverbs 6:16–19 NKJV).

In my years of living, I have watched television go from innocent to R rated. One used to question the acceptability of a cowboy movie, but now a cowboy movie seems inoffensive compared to what appears on the screen today. Immorality is just as bad today as it was in the past; the difference is that now we flaunt it. What used to be done in secret is now done in the open. The enemy is doing his job to make sin appealing to the very elite. Yet what we allow in our spirit can take root in our hearts if we are not careful. "Keep your heart with all diligence, for out of it spring the issues of life" (Proverbs 4:23 NKJV). We must be patient regarding the choices that we make in life, because the enemy is seeking those to devour. There are good choices and bad choices, and these choices are what we call matters of the heart. "Trust in the Lord with all your heart, and lean not on your own understanding; in all your ways acknowledge Him, and He shall direct your paths" (Proverbs 3:9 NKJV).

What is in our hearts will come out in our words, and eventually our words will come out in our actions. Good thoughts bear good fruit, and bad thoughts bear bad fruit, and we, the gardener, get to decide which we will have. We are the only ones with the ability to chop out the weeds in our spirit and to plant good seeds. The seeds of patience that we need in our lives are found in the Word of God.

"Be still and know that *I AM GOD*" (Psalm 46:10 NKJV). Sometime our anxious spirit gets ahead of us, and God has to remind us that we are moving without His directions. We are moving fast yet going nowhere. "Be anxious for nothing, but in everything by prayer and supplication, with thanksgiving, let your request be made known to God; and the peace of God, which surpasses all understanding, will guard your hearts and minds through Christ Jesus" (Philippians 4:6-7 NKJV).

At the moment, the world is in a crisis mode. God is getting our attention with the COVID-19 virus. God is speaking, but are we patiently listening? "If my people who are called by My name, will humble themselves, and pray and seek my face, and turn from their wicked ways; then will I hear from heaven, and will forgive their sin, and will heal their land" (2 Chronicles 7:14 NKJV). Are

God's people humbly praying and seeking God's face? We want God to heal our land, but are we willing to obey God and turn from our wicked ways? Are we willing to be intercessors who will pray for others and repent for sins that we have never committed on behalf of people we have never met? This is a personal and individual question that only God's people can answer. The world has turned far from God, but it is up to God's people, who are called by His name (*Christian*), to pray. God answers when the church begins to pray.

We look at the overall picture and say that the world is messed up. I'm not denying the facts, but it is the Christians who are held accountable. As Christians, we have not arrived at a state of perfection; this will only happen when we reach heaven. As hard as we try, we may sometimes think wrong thoughts, or maybe our words or actions at times are not loving and kind, and we find ourselves in the midst of strife and contention. Actually, this is putting it mildly, because Christians can sometimes be viciously cruel. There are Christians who have made God their Savior, but they have not made God their Lord. There is a difference when we make God our Lord, for when we make God our Lord, our hearts' desire will be that God's will is ours as well. When God's will is placed above our will, we find ourselves desiring to please God and not ourselves. We begin to seek His face and turn from our wicked ways. When that which is not godly shows up on the frontlets of our minds, we hear God's Word of instruction. "This is the right way. You should go this way" (Isaiah 30:21 NCV). We will be in tune with the convictions of God's Holy Spirit. We will not rush in where the foolish desire to go. We will patiently wait on God, who will never leave us or forsake us. "I will say of the Lord, He is my refuge and my fortress: my God, in Him will I trust. Surely He shall deliver you from the snare of the fowler and from the perilous pestilence" (Psalm 91:2-3 NKJV).

We need patience when the enemy comes against us. "Put on the whole armor of God, that you may be able to stand against the wiles of the devil" (Ephesians 6:11 NKJV). When we patiently go through tribulation, we will shine as lights in the world, knowing that the race we run is not in vain. And having patiently gone through tribulations, we gain experience that we may share with others who are going through times of trials. Our shared experience will give others hope, along with an expected end. Confidence is gained in knowing that there is hope, and hope brings light at the anticipated end of the tunnel.

Patience brings about maturity, which is a learned ability to respond to the environment in a socially appropriate manner. If we stay only as babes in Christ, we cannot be an encouragement toward others. If I never grow through trials, I will never learn the lesson that God has intended for me to learn. God is a God of purpose, and lessons are never meant to be wasted. Lessons of life are meant to grow us into the mature Christian that God would have us be. It is only through patience that we have the stamina to endure the trials. A student will never reach the point of being a teacher if they refuse to learn the lesson that is being taught, for they are still in need of learning themselves. "In fact, though by this time you ought to be teachers, you need someone to teach you the elementary truths of God's Word all over again" (Hebrews 5:12 NIV). We want to be mature teachers so that others will patiently follow us as we demonstrate through our experiences hope as the anchor for our souls. For when one does not have hope, they find despair. "Now hope does not disappoint, because the love of God has been poured out in our hearts by the Holy Spirit who was given to us" (Romans 5:5 NKJV).

Through patience, we find a peace that surpasses all knowledge. When we are surrounded by chaos, God's tender love encompasses us, and we experience an unexplainable peace. Is this peace external or internal? Perhaps when we speak of the peace of God, it is both. People sometimes vacation in a quiet cottage far away from the hustle and bustle and the turmoil of life, where they find external peace. Then there are others who quiet their minds through prayer and meditating on God's Word. And there are times when one urgently calls the name of Jesus, and a sweet peace surrounds their once anxious heart as they find internal peace. This peace is something the world cannot understand. When the external pressures of life happen, the world looks with amazement at how a Christian whose faith is in God can be so at peace—when at the same time the world views life as falling apart. When we grow in Christ, part of our growing is being able to give over to God the things that so easily beset us, for God can handle what we cannot. "Casting all your care upon Him, for He cares for you" (1 Peter 5:7 NKJV).

The internal pressures of life may rob one's peace. The Bible speaks often about strife and contention, but let us understand what is meant by these words. Strife is disagreement, and contention is arguing about the disagreement. "From whence come wars and fighting's among you? Come they not hence, even of your lusts that war in your members?" (James 4:1 KJV). One of the main causes of strife is pride. "He that is of a proud heart stirreth up strife" (Proverbs 28:25 KJV). People argue because they want to be right. But sometimes we have to give up our right so that God may be right. A fruit of the Spirit is to live a harmonious life of peace with people. "If it be possible, as much as lieth in you, live peaceably with all men" (Romans 12:18 KJV). There is peace when we pass over another's transgression. We can be wounded by someone's tactlessness—words that were unjustly spoken, an untrue rumor, or even a suspicious look. Sometimes we just have to let it go. To have peace, we must be forgivers. "And forgive us our debts, as we forgive our debtors" (Matthew 6:12 KJV). We are all subject to error, and sometimes we stumble and hurt others unintentionally, and we are in need of forgiveness. To err is human; to forgive is divine. We cannot have peace with others unless we forgive. To end a quarrel that we did not start takes forgiveness with a submissive heart.

Some Christians have grown to handle more pressure than others; they have matured in their Christian walk of faith. The one thing that used to be bothersome and looked upon as confusion is no longer a threat to one's peace of mind, for one realizes that God is not the author of confusion but of peace. For peace is not the absence of turmoil but the realization that when the waters of life are raging, we understand that it is God who created the water. No matter what is going on around us, we can experience peace because God is our peace.

Having a good conscience toward God by obeying the Spirit's commandments gives inner peace. When we do what we know is right, God gives us blessed peace. "When a man's ways please the Lord, he makes even his enemies to be at peace with him" (Proverbs 16:7 NKJV). Peace that reaches out to others is called forbearance, and it emanates from a mature, peaceable, beautiful, and merciful disposition. "With all lowliness and meekness, with longsuffering, forbearing one another in love" (Ephesians 4:2 KJV).

When we pursue peace, we unselfishly go the extra mile that inevitably demands meekness. Meekness is strength under control, for it is gentle, long-suffering, and humble. It is not domineering, blustering, or arrogant. Patience reflects a quiet and peaceful spirit that is able to work out differences and attain peaceful solutions.

Patience allows one to see the light of peace that awaits at the end of the tunnel. Patience carries you out of the darkness and into the marvelous light. "You will keep him in perfect peace, whose mind is stayed on You, because he trust in You" (Isaiah 26:3 NKJV).

The Prayer of St. Francis of Assisi

Lord, make me an instrument of your peace;
where there is hatred, let me so love;
where there is injury, pardon;
where there is discord, union;
where there is doubt, faith;
where there is despair, hope;
where there is darkness, light;
and where there is sadness, joy.

O Divine Master, grant that I may
not so much seek to be consoled,
as to console;
to be understood, as to understand;
to be loved, as to love;
for it is in giving that we receive,
it is in pardoning that we are pardoned,
and it is in dying that we are born to eternal life.
Amen. [14]

CHAPTER 6

GOD'S PATIENCE ON CALVARY

"FOR WHEN WE WERE STILL without strength, in due time Christ died for the ungodly. For scarcely for a righteous man will one die: yet perhaps for a good man some would even dare to die. But God demonstrates His own love toward us, in that while we were still sinners, Christ died for us" (Romans 5:6–8 KJV).

> When God sent forth His Son to be their Savior, men spat into the face of Jesus, plowed His back with a scourge, spiked Him naked and thorn-crowned to a tree, sneered and mocked Him in anguish until the sun hid its blushing noonday face in shame and the earth quaked in terror and the bedrock granite rent wide in protest. Yet despite it all, God has "made peace through the blood of His cross" (Colossians 1:20 KJV), surely

one of the most astounding statements in the Word of God. We could understand if it were to read that God had made war over that precious, outpoured blood and that cursed cross; but we read instead that He made peace through that very blood. God's love is incomparable.[15]

The patient love of God is manifested at Calvary, the proof of God's unconditional love toward humankind. Instead of receiving what we deserved, Jesus said, "Father, forgive them, for they know not what they do" (Luke 23:34 KJV). Christ's love on the cross is God's proof of love to the world, the church, and you and me.

A poem written by Jean Richepin depicts patient love and is titled "A Mother's Heart":

A young man gave his love to a vicious woman who demanded of him as proof of his love that he bring to her his mother's heart to feed to the dog. The young man took a knife, slew his mother, and cut out her heart. As he was running back to the evil woman, the young man stumbled and fell, and his mother's heart flew from his grasp. As it rolled by, that mother's heart was heard to cry in a still, small voice, "Are you hurt, my child, are you hurt at all?" [16]

The sweet love of God is unconditional. Even at our worst, God loves us. While we were sinners, Christ died for us. God didn't just brush us off and think of us as misfits who were constantly missing the mark. But He knew that in the fullness of time, when our eyes would be opened to the truth, we would see His patient love and draw near to Him, for it is through love and kindness that we are drawn. "Be patient therefore, brethren, unto the coming of the Lord" (James 5:7 KJV).

Sin entered into the world by one man, Adam. Death came about through sin, and death was passed down to all, for all have sinned. Prior to the coming of the law, sin was not held accountable. For there is no account kept for sin when there is no law. Adam introduced the deadly virus of sin to the world. We sin because we have been infected by sin through the carrier, Adam. But the good news is that there is a twofold antibiotic for the sin virus. The first antibiotic is the gift of God. "For God so loved the world that He gave His only begotten Son, that whoever believes in Him should not perish, but have everlasting life" (John 3:16 NKJV). Jesus is the antibiotic for sin. The second antibiotic is the grace of God. Grace is the complete cure for all our sin ills. "For by grace you have been saved through faith, and that not of yourselves; it is the gift of God" (Ephesians 2:8 NKJV). We are saved from the virus of sin by grace. Yet one will not seek a cure until they realize they are ill.

So, how does one recognize that they have a sin illness? Sin was made known by the law. "What shall we say then? Is the law sin? Certainly not! On the contrary, I would not have known sin except through the law. For I would not have known covetousness unless the law had said, 'You shall not covet'" (Romans 7:7 NKJV). The law makes sin known, and Jesus Christ is the cure for sin.

"But God demonstrates his own love for us in this: While we were still sinners, Christ died for us" (Romans 5:8 NIV). God did not just tell us that He loved us, but His love was shown through His actions. When there was absolutely nothing we could do to earn salvation, God allowed His Son to die for us. It is by God's grace, the unmerited favor of God, that we are saved. Grace is a favor that we cannot earn; nor do we even deserve it. "The wages of sin is death, but the gift of God is eternal life in Christ Jesus our Lord" (Romans 6:23 NKJV).

While we were living on the slave block of sin, God wrapped Himself in flesh and purchased us with His very own blood. He died that we may live. But the good news is He arose. God is not dead. He's alive. He arose from the grave with all power, and He is alive forevermore. The words to the song "My Redeemer Lives," sung by Nicole Mullins, express this very message. "He lives to take away my shame, He lives and forever I'll proclaim, that the payment for my sin is the very life He gave. But now He's alive and there's an empty grave. I know my redeemer lives!" Without His love and faithfulness to the cross, where would we be? "And this is the will of Him that sent Me, that everyone which sees the Son, and believes on Him, may have everlasting life" (John 6:40 NKJV).

The prophet Isaiah saw the Lord in the year that King Uzziah died. "In the year that King Uzziah died I saw the Lord sitting upon a throne, high and lifted up, and His train filled the temple" (Isaiah 6:1 KJV). King Uzziah had become stricken with leprosy after attempting to usurp the priestly duty of burning incense in the sanctuary. "Woe to those who are wise in their own eyes, and prudent in their own sight!" (Isaiah 5:21 NKJV). Although God is patient and desires that none should perish, God's love is not permissive. God does not tolerate sin, abuse, or injustice in the sense of enabling those things. "The Lord, the Lord, the compassionate and gracious God, slow to anger, abounding in love and faithfulness, maintaining love to thousands, and forgiving wickedness, rebellion and sin. Yet He does not leave the guilty unpunished" (Exodus 34:6-7 NIV).

"And even as they did not like to retain God in their knowledge, God gave them over to a reprobate mind, to do those things which are not convenient" (Romans 1:28 KJV). When a person has a reprobate mind, their conscience is no longer affected or bothered by sin. It is only for their benefit that God does not take them out of this world. God gives us time for our eyes to be opened to the truth. But how shall they know without a preacher? Before Jesus ascended from earth, He gave us the great commission to go and tell the whole earth about His saving grace, the good news of salvation. "For I am not ashamed of the gospel of Christ: for it is the power of God unto salvation to everyone that believeth" (Romans 1:16 KJV). We must tell others that salvation is free, but it was not free for Jesus; it cost His very own life. Christ died a sinner's death so that we would be set free from sin. He died that we may live.

There was nothing we could do to purchase ourselves off the slave block where we were bound in sin. And because we could not purchase ourselves, goodness and mercy that follow us all the days of our lives showed up. "Surely goodness and mercy shall follow me all the days of my life" (Psalm 23:6 KJV). Christ, who is a God of love, showed up wrapped in goodness and mercy and bought us off of the slave block for the price of His blood. Jesus purchased us with His blood, and the chains of slavery were removed. We were set free! God's patient love set us free to love others and to see others who are enslaved to sin with nonjudgmental eyes, knowing that "By the grace of God I am what I am" (1 Corinthians 15:10 KJV).

The sufferings that Christ endured to set us free were not

those of ordinary people. Christ suffered "according to the will of God" (1 Peter 4:19 NKJV). God's view of suffering is different from ours. Part of our Christian culture is desiring to know beforehand God's purpose for our suffering. In fact, we try hard to avoid being identified with the sufferings of Christ. We seek to carry out God's orders through shortcuts of our own. I hear people say, "God will never put more on you than you can bear." In fact, I have heard some people go as far as to say that this phrase is from the Bible. The truth is that God's way is always the way of suffering—the way of the *long road home.*

"Beloved, do not think it strange concerning the fiery trial which is to try you, as though some strange thing happened to you; but rejoice to the extent that you partake of Christ's sufferings, that when His glory is revealed, you may also be glad with exceeding joy" (1 Peter 4:12-13 NKJV). Are we really partakers of Christ's sufferings? Are we preparing our hearts for God to disrupt our personal ambitions? Are our hearts prepared for God to destroy our decisions through supernatural transformation? Are we prepared to walk by faith and not by sight? Through our suffering, we go through things without understanding why. Then suddenly we come to a place where our eyes are enlightened, and we realize that God has made us stronger and wiser. It is God who strengthens and anoints us. We cannot make it without God's love and His power, "For in Him we live, and move, and have our being" (Acts 17:28 KJV).

The depths of God's love in sending His Son to pay such an awful price is beyond the measure of the human mind. But we accept it with faith, or we will continually be burdened with guilt. We can never make our own atonement. We must accept the atonement that Christ has made for us. Christ took our punishment for us. It was Christ's patient love for humankind that drew Him to Calvary, and it was Calvary that drew humankind to Christ.

Cliff Barrows, a friend and associate of Billy Graham, tells this story about bearing punishment as he recalls the time he took the punishment for his children when they had disobeyed.

> They had done something I had forbidden them to do. I told them if they did the same thing again I would have to discipline them. When I returned from work and found that they hadn't minded me, the heart went out of me. I just couldn't discipline them. Bobby and Ruth were very small. I called them into my room, took off my belt and my shirt, and with a bare back, knelt down at the bed. I made them both strap me with the belt ten times each. You should have heard the crying! From them, I mean! They didn't want to do it. But I told them the penalty had to be paid and so through their sobs and tears they did what I told them.

I must admit I wasn't much of a hero. It hurt. I haven't offered to do that again, but I never had to spank them again, either, because they got the point. We kissed each other when it was over and prayed together.[17]

While we were yet sinners, God's patient love drew Jesus to Calvary. And there on Calvary, Christ paid the penalty for our sins. For only the blood of Jesus was found worthy to cover sin's cost.

Every person is important in God's eyes. That is why God is not content to stand by and watch the human race welter in misery and destruction. The greatest news of all is that humans can be born again. "For God so loved the world, that He gave His only begotten Son, that whoever believes in Him should not perish, but have everlasting life" (John 3:16 NKJV). Humans apart from God are spiritually dead. Only by God's grace through faith in Christ can this new birth take place.

CHAPTER 7

GOD'S LOVE REWARDS PATIENCE

"REJOICE AND BE EXCEEDINGLY GLAD, for great is your reward in heaven" (Matthew 5:12 KJV). "If we endure, we will also reign with Him. If we disown Him, He will also disown us" (2 Timothy 2:12 NIV). God's patience is given as a cause for reward. "If in this life only we have hope in Christ, we are of all men most miserable" (1 Corinthians 15:19 KJV). Our suffering is not in vain. If we suffer with Him, we will reign with Him. One day, we shall see Him face-to-face, and we shall behold His glory. God has promised us eternal life and that the suffering of this present day will soon pass away. The justness for suffering will be found in the next life. "The righteous will be glad when they are avenged, when they dip their feet in the blood of the wicked. Then people will say, 'Surely the righteous still are rewarded; surely there is a God who judges the earth" (Psalm 58:10–11 NIV).

Suffering causes us to discipline our minds by focusing on our hope, which is the grace that will be revealed at the revelation of Jesus Christ. "That the trial of your faith, being much more precious than of gold that perisheth, though it be tried with fire, might be found unto praise and honor and glory at the appearing of Jesus Christ" (1 Peter 1:7 KJV). We shall behold Him in all His glory! Philip Yancey put it this way: "No one is exempt from tragedy or disappointment—God Himself was not exempt. Jesus offered no immunity, no way out of the unfairness, but rather a way through it to the other side."[18]

A man who lost his wife and children in a terrible accident penned the words to this song:

> When peace like a river attendeth my way!
> When sorrows like a sea billows roll:
> Whatever my lot, You have taught me to say,
> "It is well, it is well with my soul."[19]

"Then Jesus said to His disciples, 'If anyone desires to come after Me, let him deny himself, and take up his cross, and follow Me" (Matthew 16:24 NKJV). As Christians, we all have a cross to bear. In Psalms 42:5, 11 and 43:5 (NCV), the same question is asked three times. "Why am I so sad? Why am I so upset? I should put my hope in God and keep praising Him, my Savior and my God." Rather than dwelling on the hurt, we must place focus on our God! In the book of Job, when Job submitted to God, he said, "My ears had heard of You before, but now my eyes have seen You" (Job 42:5 NCV). Having a vision of God is the source of patience. Our true and proper inspiration of God comes when we see Him. Seeing God makes us take a step backward, causing us to pause and ponder who God really is!

In Sheila Walsh's book *Holding on to Heaven with Hell on Your Back*, she tells the story of Bob Wieland, who went to Vietnam standing six feet tall and weighing 270 pounds. Bob came home two feet, ten and a half inches tall and weighing eighty-seven pounds after a Viet Cong mine blew him in half. Those who found him thought he was dead. But with an inward motivation, he began to strengthen his upper body to the point that he could lift 340 pounds. With this strength, he entered a weight lifting contest and won. With much regret, he was disqualified after the rules stated that he must have shoes on. Through his disappointment, he remembered his first thought when he came to in Vietnam: "*Well, Lord, they tried to finish me off here, but I'm still alive. So what do You want me to do? What purpose do You have for my life?"* [20] Our hope in Christ empowers us to come to God with open hands, into which He can place what He wants and out of which He can take what should not be there.

When life seems utterly overwhelming and you can't understand its purpose, "He makes me lie down in green pastures, He leads me beside quiet waters, He refreshes my soul" (Psalm 23:2-3 NIV). It is in quiet serenity that God brings newness to the chaos of life, and we become confident of this: "I would have lost heart, unless I had believed that I would see the goodness of the Lord in the land of the living. Wait on the Lord; be of good courage, and He shall strengthen your heart; wait I say on the Lord!" (Psalm 27:13-14 NKJV). We must look to God and put our trust in Him. "I will lift up mine eyes unto the hills, from whence cometh my help. My help comes from the Lord, which made heaven and earth" (Psalms 121:1-2 KJV).

Waiting does not mean sitting idly by but actively doing the instructions of God and not getting ahead of Him. I've gone to restaurants where waiters stand close by with a towel across their arm, waiting for any sign that shows their help is needed, yet also making sure they are not in the way. That is how we wait on God, by actively doing what He calls us to do and not what we have called ourselves to do.

Throughout the day, we listen for God's voice of direction that guides us to check on someone through a phone call or a hospital visit. Or maybe God leads us to send a birthday card or a get-well card in order to cheer up someone. But all the while, we listen for God's directives so that we will not overstep our boundaries with others by being over impulsive or intruding where we should not go. We overstep boundaries with people when we sometimes do things that we have not been asked to do. There are people who do not want help unless they ask for it, and there are people who would like help but do not know how to ask. As we wait on God, He gives us a spirit of discernment to know the difference. God will never lead us wrong, and His directives are never the same, but they are always consistent. We listen for His still, small voice that tells us to go to the right or to the left, and it is to this voice that we must willingly obey.

After working more than twenty years for a company, my husband, whose name is Billy, decided to start his own business. As his wife, I backed him up and quit my full-time job to help work the business. His plans were to continue working his full-time job until the business financially exceeded his income as well as the income that I was making from my previous job.

We started the company, Precise Test Lab, Inc. (PTL) in an incubator that was designed to help small businesses. Billy purchased used equipment and made the best out of everything. He made sure that the facility and all the equipment were clean and in proper working condition.

At that time, the business was totally foreign to me. Actually, I have come to realize that not many people truly understand the logistics of the service that we provide, which is nondestructive testing (NDT). The main responsibility of nondestructive testing is to safely protect the general public, for the world would be chaos without it. And although most people have never heard of the practice of NDT, you have probably encountered it while going through an x-ray scanner at an airport or if you have ever had an MRI. While NDT comes in about twenty forms, PTL performs three classis types: fluorescent penetrant inspection, radiography inspection, and magnetic particle inspection. Fluorescent penetrant inspection is used to detect surface discontinuities and is characterized by the ability to fluoresce when under ultraviolet illumination (black light). Radiography inspection detects internal discontinuities in materials by the use of x-ray or gamma ray.

Magnetic particle inspection is an NDT method that uses very small magnetic particles to reveal discontinuities in parts that are capable of being magnetized. Although NDT is used for many functions, even detecting foreign objects in baby food, PTL's focus is the aerospace arena. PTL certifies that planes are safe, thereby preventing them from falling out of the sky.

After one year of being in business, we made a grand total of sixty dollars. This was definitely not a get-rich-quick business. One day, after feeling very defeated, Billy walked outside and took a towel, with the intention of throwing it in and giving up. He slung the towel over his shoulder to really throw it in, and the towel fell on the ground behind him. That was Billy's confirmation from the Lord to keep going and not give up. That day, Billy promised the Lord that if He opened up the doors of opportunity for him, he would not let God down.

During the time that business was slow, I was trying to wrap my head around what we were actually doing. In fact, the way I felt, I might as well have been writing procedures for a foreign language. However, I did not let that stop me; I knew that, with God and patience, I could do all things.

Billy thought big and knew that if we were going to do things on a large scale, we had to conduct business with large corporations.

With that mindset, he contacted major corporations in hopes that we would be placed on their supplier list. He was told by representatives that we had to prove that our services were needed in the area. In order to prove that, a large corporation would have to contact a major corporation and state that there was a need for an NDT laboratory in the area. After many phone calls, Billy convinced a large corporation to contact one of their major sources, stating that our services would be an asset to their business.

Shortly after this, we received a phone call that provided us with a date for an upcoming audit at our place of business, located inside a small business incubator. The staff at the incubator was happy for us, and it became a big deal. The manager began painting the entry walls, trying to make everything presentable.

The day finally arrived for our audit. The audit was very stressful, and when it was all over and the findings were reviewed, things did not look very good. Yet we were determined to do better, as we were given thirty days to right the wrong. We energetically pushed, and we conquered everything on the list to the best of our ability. We conscientiously did the very best we could.

Hard work does pay off. When the corporation returned to check the corrected findings, to our thrilled amazement, we were told that we had passed the audit. In fact, not only did we pass the audit, but soon afterward, major companies started sending work to our facility for NDT testing. As Billy patiently waited on God, he knew in his heart that God desires for us to think big, because He is *a big God!*

One day while going over a bank statement, because at the time I was also the accountant, I noticed an unfamiliar deposit to our account that I had no recollection of. I contacted the bank to notify them of a discrepancy for an overage of $3,000. The bank told me that they would check into the matter and get back with me. A few days later, the bank called to thank me for notifying them. I was told that the money that was accidently deposited into our account was not $3,000; it was $3 million. I was flabbergasted, for it never crossed my mind to pay attention to how many zeros followed the number three. The bank stated that it would have taken them along time to find the error, but eventually they would have. In my heart, I felt that it was a test from God to see if He could trust us with riches. The business exceeded far beyond what we could have ever asked for or even thought of. Success comes with the price of hard work and patience. If a man wants to eat, he must work.

Starting the business was not easy. At one point, I could not even turn my neck due to the strain of writing the various necessary procedures, along with implementing the important business documents that pertain to NDT. Billy was also feeling the strain of working both his outside job and the business. God instructs us to be patient, yet He never promises a rose garden.

The income from the business finally succeeded Billy's salary, even after hiring extra help. Billy walked away from his other job, which up until then had been our bread and butter. It was time to totally depend on God, who is our Provider. Patiently working hard serves God in a manner that is honorable.

As we patiently climbed the ladder of success, we moved from the incubator into a new, custom-built 15,000-square-foot facility with all new state-of-the-art equipment. Billy continued to work long hours, and at the close of each day, Billy locked the doors and gave God thanks for another day of hard work. When much is given, much is required.

We were patiently making history. Who would have ever thought that with patience and the grace of God, our test facility would be an innovative part of Blue Origin, whose plans are to send a woman and another man to the moon by 2024. To God be the glory!

"For we walk by faith, not by sight" (2 Corinthians 5:7 NKJV). Through faith, we go as far as we can go, and then we take one more step, and that step is called the step of faith. There are times when God calls us to do things, and our minds question, *Is this God?* This is when we stop thinking with our minds and we listen to our hearts and take a step of faith. It may be a time when God calls us to visit someone who is sick, and we call before we go, but there is no answer, yet still we follow our hearts and go anyway, only to find that the person we went to visit had fallen and could not get to the phone. When we wait on God, our hearts' desire must be to serve Him the best we can. God looks at the heart, and there is no pretending with God; He sees through phoniness. That is why we are to worship God in spirit and in truth. God lets us know right up front, "Do not pretend with Me, because *I Am God*, who knows all things and sees all things." We may sometimes fool people, but we will never fool God. We must come to God straight up.

God is a God who cares and is concerned with our everyday lives, and not only that—He is a God who sustains us and keeps us among the chaos of this world. Therefore, we do not go through suffering as one who has no hope. Patience also means cheerful or hopeful endurance under suffering in faith and duty. God does not intend for us to go through suffering with our heads always hung down. When our hope is in Christ, "We are perplexed, but not in despair; persecuted, but not forsaken; struck down, but not destroyed" (2 Corinthians 4:8-9 NKJV). "The joy of the Lord is your strength" (Nehemiah 8:10 KJV). We are not to run from our situations, nor are we to fear, but we are to hold our heads high, staying strong in our faith, knowing that God is going through our situation with us. "Be joyful in hope, patient in affliction, faithful in prayer" (Romans 12:12 NIV).

We must learn to dance in the rain. God's Holy Spirit strengthens us so that joyfulness is displayed through patience. "And let us not be weary in well doing: for in due season we shall reap, if we faint not" (Galatians 6:9 KJV). God's Word teaches us not to give up, and when we abide in His Word, God will keep us in the trials that come to test us.

I recently heard a story about a man by the name of Ray Hinton; he was acquitted after spending thirty years on death row for a crime he did not commit. God kept him from being wrongly executed. Thirty innocent years on death row is a long time to be tested, but God kept him. Some people would have lost their mind through it all. But if your mind is stayed on Christ, your faith in God will sustain you. "Fear none of those things which thou shalt suffer: behold, the devil shall cast some of you into prison, that ye may be tried; and ye shall have tribulation ten days: be thou faithful unto death, and I will give thee a crown of life" (Revelation 2:10 KJV). Ray Hinton was acquitted, yet for those who are innocent and the sentence of death is given, Jesus welcomes them with a crown of life. Those who love the Lord and endure the testing win, no matter what the outcome. The Lord has promised us the crown of life, and God is a promise keeper. He is a rewarder for those who diligently seek Him. "Trust in the Lord with all your heart; and lean not on your own understanding. In all your ways acknowledge Him and He shall direct your path" (Proverbs 3:5-6 KJV). We must always trust God, whether things make sense or not. God already knows the outcome, so why try to do things our own way without the security of knowing the future? It's like trusting in the wind; we never know which way it's going to blow. John Blanchard once said, "Walking by faith means being prepared to trust where we are not permitted to see."

We must stay connected to God in order to hear from Him, and the way we stay connected is through prayer. "Call to Me and I will answer you, and show you great and mighty things which you do not know" (Jeremiah 33:3 NKJV). God wants to show us things, but we must first call on Him in prayer. God is omniscient. He knows all things, and there is nothing hidden from Him. We in our finite minds are limited in our knowledge no matter how brainy we think we are. Why would one desire to plan their own steps when God says, "Obey my voice, and I will be your God, and you shall be my people. And walk in all the ways that I have commanded you, that it may be well with you" (Jeremiah 7:23 NKJV)? God has a plan and a purpose for each of us. We must live patiently, taking one second, one minute, and one day at a time. Life is not a sprint but a marathon.

The fastest runner does not always win the race, but time and chance happen to us all. Stop pacing the floor and rest in God. I have heard it said, "Let go and let God." We cannot fix what we do not know is broken, for that is like chasing the wind, which is futile. Sometimes one must pray, *Lord, calm my anxious spirit.* We worry and fret about what we do not know, yet worrying will never change a thing but the color of our hair. But oh how peaceful is patience; it is like a breath of fresh air on a warm spring day; it is like snuggling up with God when the world is spinning out of control.

When we trust in God and patiently stand on His promises, allowing our hearts to say, "Yes, Lord, I will trust in You," then the peace of God, which surpasses all knowledge, will overtake us like a flood, and we can say, "It is well with my soul!"

CHAPTER 8

GOD'S PATIENT LOVE NEVER ENDS

"BEHOLD, I SHOW YOU A mystery: We shall not all sleep, but we shall all be changed, in a moment, in the twinkling of an eye, at the last trump. For the trumpet shall sound, and the dead shall be raised incorruptible, and we shall be changed. For this corruptible must put on incorruption, and this mortal must put on immortality. So when this corruptible shall have put on incorruption, and this mortal shall have put on immorality, then shall be brought to pass the saying that is written, death is swallowed up in victory. O death, where is thy sting? O grave, where is thy victory?" (1 Corinthians 15:51–55 KJV).

One day a little boy was riding in the car with his father when a bee flew in through the window and started buzzing around the boy. He began to scream, "The bee is going to sting me!" But his father reached out and grabbed the bee. He held it in his hand for a few seconds, then released it.

The bee began to buzz around, and the boy started to cry again. But his father said, "Son, you don't have to be afraid. All the bee can do is make noise." Then the dad held out his hand, and there in the palm of his hand was the bee's stinger.

On the cross of Calvary, Jesus Christ took the stinger of sin, which is death. So all death can do now is make noise.[21]

The victory has already been won. The sting is sin, and Jesus conquered sin through His death, and by His resurrection from the grave, the sting was removed. Death and the grave lost to the victory of Christ!

Yet there are some who continue to ask, "If a man die, shall he live again?" (Job 14:14 KJV). Some people challenge the Christian belief of an afterlife by saying that death is the end. If there is no afterlife, then the Christian message is a lie, Christ's death is merely wasted blood, and Christians are the most pitiable of all people. Jesus's resurrection from the dead gave the world decisive proof that God has the power and the will to overcome death. Death, which is known as the enemy, is the last enemy to be destroyed and finally conquered, thereby becoming not an end but a beginning.

"Let not your heart be troubled; you believe in God, believe also in Me. In My Father's house are many mansions; if it were not so, I would have told you. I go to prepare a place for you. And if I go and prepare a place for you, I will come again and receive you to Myself; that where I am, there you may be also" (John 14:1-3 KJV).

Don Piper, in his book *90 Minutes in Heaven*, tells the story of his drive home one afternoon that ended in a head-on collision, where he was within minutes pronounced dead. At the scene of the crash was a pastor by the name of Dick Onerecker, who said that he was led by the Holy Spirit to pray for the man under the tarp who was dead and lying there in a messed-up condition. Dick crawled in the car behind Don and began to pray fervently and to sing. Ninety minutes after Don was pronounced dead, Don began to join Dick in singing the song "What a Friend We Have in Jesus." Talk about somebody scrambling out of a car at record speed—that was Dick. In Don Piper's book, he tells his true story of what happened during his ninety minutes in heaven. I would like to share a short excerpt of Dick's time spent in heaven:

> I just didn't hear music. It seemed as if I were part of the music—and it played through my body. ... The praise was unending ... hundreds of songs were being sung at the same time—all of them worshiping God. ... "Hallelujah!" "Praise!" "Glory

to God!" "Praise to the King!" Such words rang out in the midst of all the music. ... Every sound blended, and each voice or instrument enhanced the others. ... I heard no sad songs and instinctively knew that there are no sad songs in heaven. ... All were praises about Christ's reign as King of Kings and our joyful worship for all He has done for us and how wonderful He is.

... In those minutes—and, they held no sense of time for me—others touched me, and their warm embraces were absolutely real. I saw colors I would never have believe existed. I've never, ever felt more alive than I did then. I was home; I was where I belonged, I wanted to be there more than I had ever wanted to be anywhere on earth. Time had slipped away, and I was simply present in heaven. All worries, anxieties, and concerns vanished, I had no needs, and I felt perfect.[22]

"Then I looked again, and I heard the singing of thousands and millions of angels around the throne and the living beings and the elders" (Revelation 5:11 NLT). How wonderful it is to sing praises to God; singing here on earth is only a taste of what is in store for us in heaven. "But as it is written: Eye has not seen, nor ear heard, nor have entered into the heart of man the things which God has prepared for those who love Him" (1 Corinthians 2:9 NKJV).

There have been numerous people who have experienced the afterlife and come back to tell their story. Yet many people do not believe in life after death, and they are filled with pessimism, darkness, and tragedy. Jesus said, "I am the resurrection, and the life. He who believes in Me, though he may die, he shall live. And whoever lives and believes in Me shall never die. Do you believe this?" (John 11:25-26 NKJV). Our hope of immorality is not based on desires, longings, arguments, or instincts; our hope of immorality is based on Christ alone. Paul in the New Testament declared the resurrection in this manner: "Moreover, brethren, I declare unto you the gospel which I preached unto you, which also you have received, and wherein you stand; by which also you are saved, if you keep in memory what I preached unto you, unless you have believed in vain. For I delivered unto you first of all that which I also received, how that Christ died for our sins according to the scriptures; and that he was buried, and that he rose again the third day according to the scriptures" (1 Corinthians 15:1-4 KJV).

The Bible makes the way to heaven clear, yet some would like to think they have a better way. Such is the case with the conversation between Auguste Comte, the French philosopher, and Thomas Carlyle, the Scottish essayist:

> Comte declared his intention of starting a new religion that would supplant entirely the religion of Christ. It was to have no mysteries, was to be plain as the multiplication table, and its name was

to be positivism. "Very good, Mr. Comte," Carlyle replied, "very good. All you will need to do will be to speak as never a man spake, and live as never a man lived, and be crucified and rise again the third day, and get the world to believe that you are still alive. Then your religion will have a chance to get on."[23]

If you trust the resurrected Christ as your Lord and Savior, He will be with you when you die and will give you life with Him forever. "Lo, I am with you always, even unto the end of the world" (Matthew 28:20 KJV). Christ's guarantee is that: life has a new meaning. The disciples were in despair after the crucifixion. They said, "We had hoped that he was the one who was going to redeem Israel" (Luke 24:21 NIV). They were full of anguish because they thought of Christ's death as such a tragedy. Life had lost its meaning for them. But when He rose from the grave, they saw the living Christ, and life took on purpose once more.

Through faith in Jesus, we possess heaven. On earth, through patience, we possess our souls. After Jesus told His disciples that they would be hated by all men for His name's sake and promised them that they would not be harmed, He said, "In your patience possess ye your souls" (Luke 21:19 KJV). Possessing your soul is accomplished through the process of sanctification, a renewing of the mind. Our minds need to be saved. We can have a new life and a new heart but have an old mind. We can have a heart full of love yet lack spiritual insight. The intents of our hearts can be pure, but our heads can be confused. We must come to the foot of the cross with a willingness to forsake traditional mentalities and trust God for a new mind. If we do our part, even if we do not know how, God will do His. Our former thought processes and prejudices must be altered. "Let this mind be in you, which was also in Christ Jesus" (Philippians 2:5 KJV). We cannot use our old brain to accept spiritual truth, because an unrenewed mentality is spiritually dead, and anyone possessing spiritual discernment will be aware that it is dead.

The mind gives rise to wisdom, knowledge, and reasoning. Our emotions allow us to express love or hate, joy or anger, happiness or sadness. These elements connect humanness to the soul. No person's words are entirely trustworthy, for what a person says and how they conduct themselves may be holy, but their thought pattern may not be spiritual. So what we observe of a person is their mind. Therefore a person's heart may be renewed, but their mind has remained old. God wants to restore our thought life to the state in which we were first created so that we may glorify God in our walk and also in our thinking. "And be not conformed to this world:

but be ye transformed by the renewing of your mind, that you may prove what is that good, and acceptable, and perfect, will of God" (Romans 12:2 KJV).

People do not automatically turn to God's will; they have full power to decide for themselves. They possess their own volition to choose to follow God's will or to resist Him and follow Satan's will instead. The will determines whether the spirit, the body, or the soul rules. "For it is God which worketh in you both to will and to do His good pleasure" (Philippians 2:13 KJV). God desires that the spirit should control the whole being, but the will part of the individual belongs to the soul. The soul is master of all actions, for the body follows its direction.

The soul is the personality; the will, intellect and emotion. The soul is the axis of the entire being, because a person's volition belongs to it. Volition is the instrument through which we make decisions, and it is expressed through our willingness or unwillingness. When the soul is willing to assume a humble position, the spirit will then be able to manage the whole person. If the soul rebels against taking a humble position, the spirit will be powerless to rule. Such is the meaning of free will.

"For ye have need of patience, that, after ye have done the will of God, ye might receive the promise" (Hebrews 10:36 KJV).

We patiently wait for the promise by trusting in God and leaning not on our own understanding. We take time to meditate on the goodness of Jesus—His death, burial, and resurrection—with the realization that because He lives, we too will live again.

"The Lord is not slack concerning His promises, as some men count slackness; but is long-suffering to us-ward, not willing that any should perish, but that all should come to repentance" (2 Peter 3:9 KJV). We must consider that the long-suffering of our Lord is salvation. "May God Himself, the God of peace, sanctify you through and through. May your whole spirit, soul and body be kept blameless at the coming of our Lord Jesus Christ" (1 Thessalonians 5:23 NIV). We as Christians have the full assurance of hope until the end. "For yet a little while, and He who is coming will come, and will not tarry" (Hebrews 10:37 KJV).

Yet "some will abandon the faith and follow deceiving spirits and things taught by demons. Such teachings come through hypocritical liars, whose consciences have been seared" (1 Timothy 4:1-2 NIV). We need to be rooted and grounded in the truth. We do this by studying the Word of God so that we will not be ashamed as we rightly divide the Word of truth. When we stand on God's Word, we are standing on His promises. If we do not stand on His Word, we will fall for anything. "Therefore let him who thinks he stands take heed lest he fall" (1 Corinthians 10:12 NKJV).

Although God is all-powerful and has the ability to wipe out entire nations through their disobedience, God loves us and is willing that none should perish. God patiently withholds His wrath because He knows that we were made from dust. "For I am persuaded, that neither death, nor life, nor angels, nor principalities, nor powers, nor things present, nor things to come, nor height, nor depth, nor any other creature, shall be able to separate us from the love of God, which is in Christ Jesus our Lord" (Romans 8:38–39 KJV).

The Bible speaks of the marriage supper of the Lamb, that we are to be ready and prepared for the return of Christ, as He will return and usher us into the presence of God to live eternally. I've heard it said that everybody talks about going to heaven, but nobody wants to die. When we realize the truth about heaven, we will not fear death. And when we have conquered the last enemy, which is death, we will be able to say, "O death, where is thy sting? O grave, where is thy victory?" (1 Corinthians 15:55 KJV).

When my father, whose name was John, was dying and about to be ushered into the presence of Jesus, I read these words to him: "And I John saw the holy city, new Jerusalem, coming down from

God out of heaven, prepared as a bride adorned for her husband" (Revelation 21:2 KJV). What comforting assurance it is to know with certainty that God's words are true and faithful. "Let not your heart be troubled; you believe in God, believe also in Me. In My Father's house are many mansions; if it were not so, I would have told you. I go to prepare a place for you. And if I go and prepare a place for you, I will come again and receive you to Myself; that where I am, there you may be also" (John 14:1-3 NKJV). The Bible uses the universal beauty of a bride to describe heaven. "And God shall wipe away all tears from their eyes: and there shall be no more death, neither sorrow, nor crying, neither shall there be no more pain: for the former things are passed away. And he that sat upon the throne said, Behold, I make all things new" (Revelation 21:4-5 KJV).

> There are those today who say that we must do as others do, that we must conform to our world, that we must swim with the tide, that we must move with the crowd. But the believer says: "No, do not expect me to fall in with the evil customs and ways of this world. I am in Rome, but I will not do as Rome does. I am an alien, a stranger, and a foreigner. My citizenship is in heaven."[24]

We are still in the age of God's patient grace. The forgiveness that God offers still stands. "Enter through the narrow gate. For wide is the gate and broad is the road that leads to destruction, and many enter through it. But small is the gate and narrow the road that leads to life, and only a few find it" (Matthew 7:13-14 NIV). The Bible continues to warn that one day the door will be closed, and it will be too late. "Now is the accepted time" (2 Corinthians 6:2 KJV). Accept the Lord's patient offer of forgiveness today, for tomorrow may very well be too late. Jesus tells us that there is only one way to heaven: "I am the way and the truth and the life. No one comes to the Father except through me" (John 14:6 NKJV). Jesus patiently stands at the doors of our hearts, knocking. "Behold, I stand at the door, and knock: if any man hear my voice, and open the door, I will come in to him, and will sup with him, and he with me" (Revelation 3:20 KJV).

While taking family road trips, there have been numerous times when I have found myself stuck in traffic for hours due to construction along the way. When I finally arrive at the end of the construction, I am ever so grateful to see a sign that reads: "End of Construction—Thank You for Your Patience!" As Christians, when we reach the end of life's journey here on earth and reflect back over our lives, we will thankfully say, "Thank You, God, for Your patience!" But until then, God patiently sees us as a work still in progress. Life is not a sprint but a marathon.

NOTES

1   Leroy Brownlow, *The Fruit of the Spirit* (Fort Worth: Brownlow Publishing Company, 1982), 12.

2   Eric Metaxas, *Bonhoeffer* (Nashville: Thomas Nelson, 2010), 458.

3   Brownlow, *The Fruit of the Spirit*, 46.

4   Charles R. Swindoll, *The Tale of the Tardy Oxcart* (Nashville: Word Publishing, 1998), 425-27.

5   Max Lucado, *God Came Near* (Portland: Multnomah Press, 1987) 30-31.

6   Brownlow, *The Fruit of the Spirit*, 15-16.

7   Brother Yun and Paul Hattaway, *The Heavenly Man* (London: Monarch Books, 2002), 112-13.

8   Joni Erickson Tada and Steven Estes, *When God Weeps* (Grand Rapids: Zondervan Publishing House, 1997), 127.

9   Millard J. Erickson, *Christian Theology Second Edition* (Grand Rapids: Baker Books, 1983), 1247.

10 Tada, *When God Weeps*, 196-97.

11 Tada, 21.

12 Reinhold Nicbuhr, *Serenity Prayer* (Wikipedia, s.v. "Serenity Prayer," last modified December 26, 2020, 09:40, https://en.wikepedia.org/wiki/Serenity_Prayer).

13 Darlene Bishop, *Your Life Follows Your Words* (Denver: Legacy Publishers International, 2004), 79.

14 Anonymous, *Prayer of St. Francis of Assisi* (en.m.wikisource.org, 2020).

15 John Phillips, *Exploring Romans* (Grand Rapids: Kregel Publications, 2002), 92.

16 Phillips, 91.

17 Billy Graham, *How to Be Born Again* (Waco: Word Books Publisher, 1977), 116.

18 Philip Yancey, *Disappointment with God* (Grand Rapids: Zondervan Publishing House, 1998), 186.

19 The National Baptist Hymnal, *It Is Well with My Soul* (Nashville: National Baptist Publishing Board, February 1980), 189.

20 Sheila Walsh, *Holding on to Heaven with Hell on Your Back* (Nashville: Thomas Nelson Publishers, 1990), 202.

21 Tony Evans, *The Best Is Yet to Come* (Chicago: Moody Press, 2000), 236.

22 Don Piper and Cecil Murphey, *90 Minutes in Heaven* (Grand Rapids: Fleming H. Revell, 2004), 40-44.

23 Graham, *How to be Born Again,*133.

24 Billy Graham, *World Aflame* (Garden City: Doubleday & Company, Inc., 1965), 261.

BIBLIOGRAPHY

Alexander, Joseph Addison. *A Guide to Christian Workers-KJV Bible.* Nashville: Thomas Nelson, 2017.

Bishop, Darlene. *Your Life Follows Your Words.* Denver: Legacy Publishers International, 2004.

Brownlow, Leroy. *The Fruit of the Spirit.* Fort Worth: Brownlow Publishing Company, 1982.

Evans, Tony. *The Best Is Yet to Come.* Chicago: Moody Press, 2000.

Graham, Billy. *How to Be Born Again.* Waco: Word Books Publisher, 1977.

Graham, Billy. *World Aflame.* Garden City: Doubleday & Company, 1965.

Ilibagiza, Immaculée, and Steven Ervin. *Left to Tell.* Carlsbad: Hay House Inc., 2006.

Jackson, Catherine. *The Christian's Secret of a Happy Life for Today*. Minneapolis: Fleming H. Revell Company, 1979.

Lucado, Max. *God Came Near*. Portland: Multnomah Press, 1987.

Metaxas, Eric. *Bonhoeffer*. Nashville: Thomas Nelson, 2010.

Phillips, John. *Exploring Romans*. Grand Rapids: Kregel Publications, 2002.

Piper, Don and Cecil Murphey. *90 Minutes in Heaven*. Grand Rapids: Fleming H. Revell, 2004.

Swindoll, Charles R. *The Tale of the Tardy Oxcart*. Nashville: Word Publishing, 1998.

Tada, Joni Erickson and Steven Estes. *When God Weeps*. Grand Rapids: Zondervan Publishing House, 1997.

Walsh, Sheila. *Holding on to Heaven with Hell on Your Back*. Nashville: Thomas Nelson Publishers, 1990.

Yancey, Phillip. *Disappointment with God*. Grand Rapids: Zondervan Publishing House, 1998.

Yun, Brother and Paul Hattaway. *The Heavenly Man*. London: Monarch Books, 2002.

ABOUT THE AUTHOR

DR. YONNIE FOWLER (Bachelor Degree in Family Life Education from Spring Arbor University; Master and Doctorate Degree in Ministry of the Bible from Covington Theological Seminary). Yonnie was born in Jackson, Michigan, where she resides with her husband Billy whom she married in 1971. They have one son and two daughters and are enjoying the addition of grandchildren. She attends Second Missionary Baptist Church.

Printed in the United States
by Baker & Taylor Publisher Services